# Hwa Yu T'ai Chi Ch'uan

Hwa Yu Grand Master John Chung Li.

# Hwa Yu T'ai Chi Ch'uan

*Unlocking the Mysteries of the*
*Five-Word Song*

## Glenn D. Newth

Photography by Mark Newth & Johnson Photo Imaging

Foreword by
**Robert F. Xavier, Ph.D.**

Blue Snake Books
Berkeley, California

Published by Blue Snake Books/Frog, Ltd.
Blue Snake Books/Frog, Ltd. books are distributed by
North Atlantic Books
P.O. Box 12327
Berkeley, California 94712

Cover and book design by Susan Quasha
Cover and interior chinese calligraphy by Guoqiang Shi
Printed in the United States of America

Blue Snake Books' publications are available through most bookstores. For further information, call 800-337-2665 or visit our websites at www.northatlanticbooks.com or www.bluesnakebooks.com.

Substantial discounts on bulk quantities are available to corporations, professional associations, and other organizations. For details and discount information, contact our special sales department.

PLEASE NOTE: The creators and publishers of this book disclaim any liabilities for loss in connection with following any of the practices, exercises, and advice contained herein. To reduce the chance of injury or any other harm, the reader should consult a professional before undertaking this or any other martial arts, movement, meditative arts, health, or exercise program. The instructions and advice printed in this book are not in any way intended as a substitute for medical, mental, or emotional counseling with a licensed physician or health-care provider.

Library of Congress Cataloging-in-Publication Data

Newth, Glenn D., 1953–
    Hwa yu tai chi ch'uan : unlocking the mysteries of the five word song
/ by Glenn D. Newth ; photography by Mark Newth & Johnson Photo Imaging.
        p. cm.
    Summary: "A complete philosophical, theoretical, and practical guide
to the Hwa Yu Tai Chi Ch'uan (a temple style), and its unique and
sophisticated kinesthetic practice form that promotes optimal health and
dynamic hand fighting skills"—Provided by publisher.
    ISBN-13: 978-1-58394-161-4 (trade paper)
    ISBN-10: 1-58394-161-4 (trade paper)
    1. Tai chi.    I. Title.
GV504.N49 2006
613.7'148—dc22
2006010174

1 2 3 4 5 6 7 8 9 UNITED 12 11 10 09 08 07 06

**I would like to dedicate this book in memory of the late Grand Master, John Chung Li**

I would also like to express my personal thanks and appreciation to the
following individuals for their selfless contributions,
whether large or small,
in making this project a reality:

Karen Borla

Mark Newth

Cory Newth

Beverly Brylow

Mary McNaughton

John Phillips

The staff at Johnson Photo Imaging

Guoqiang Shi

Robert Kennedy

... and a special thanks to Master Robert Xavier

# Contents

FOREWORD BY ROBERT F. XAVIER, PH.D.      ix

INTRODUCTION      xi

**Chapter 1: Hwa Yu T'ai Chi and Its Ancient Health Secrets**      1

*An introduction to Hwa Yu T'ai Chi, its founders, its origins, and its many health and self-defense benefits.*

**Chapter 2: The Structure of Hwa Yu**      13

*The different components of Hwa Yu, and the step-by-step process of learning the art.*

**Chapter 3: The Six Combinations and Eight Methods & The Five-Word Song**      23

*A full recounting of and commentary on the Six Combinations and Eight Methods, key elements of Hwa Yu T'ai Chi's philosophy, and a translation of Hwa Yu's Five-Word Song.*

**Chapter 4: The History of Hwa Yu**      41

*The history and lineage of Hwa Yu T'ai Chi, from ancient times to the present.*

**Chapter 5: Warm-Ups and Rooting Exercises**      49

*An introduction to warm-up and stretching exercises, and illustrated instruction in the three important Hwa Yu rooting exercises of Rowing, Walking, and Standing.*

**Chapter 6: The Hwa Yu Long Form: General Instructions & Sections One and Two of the Form**      73

*A discussion of the theories and concepts that make Hwa Yu an effective form of combat and self-defense. Theories and principles for practicing the first two sections of the Hwa Yu long form, with photos of the movements and their self-defense applications.*

**Chapter 7: The Long Form: Sections Three, Four, and Five**      123

*Continuation of form explanations, with photos of each movement.*

**Chapter 8: The Animal Forms and Push Hands**      151

*An explanation of the Animal Forms and the Push Hands exercise, including a demonstration of the Crane Form and its self-defense application.*

RECOMMENDED READING      **159**

ABOUT THE AUTHOR      **160**

# Foreword

Hwa Yu T'ai Chi has evolved from its ninth-century Chinese origins into a highly advanced exercise program, which promotes healing and general well-being. Hidden from the world until the last fifty years, Hwa Yu T'ai Chi was practiced only by the elite: the nobility, the rulers, and the palace guards. Hwa Yu is accepted as the oldest temple-style, closed-door healthcare science—some of the 1,000-year-old skills defined in this book have never before been revealed!

Hwa Yu T'ai Chi is one of the world's most unique martial arts systems. It incorporates principles that became three of the most versatile and effective internal Chinese martial arts in practice today: Pa Kua Chang, Hsing I Ch'uan, and t'ai chi ch'uan. Most importantly, the current principles of Hwa Yu still adhere strictly to the ancient Five-Word Song, the art's original doctrine: In over one thousand years, no movement principle has been left open to personal interpretation. What's more, Hwa Yu T'ai Chi self-defense methods have been field-tested and used by professional martial artists to standardize defensive tactics for law enforcement throughout the country.

For many centuries, knowledgeable taoist masters and healers have recommended Hwa-Yu T'ai Chi for the prevention, treatment, and reversal of a wide range of common disorders. It is believed to strengthen the immune system, and, therefore aid in prevention and care of such afflictions as heart disease, Alzheimer's, and cancer. Hwa Yu helps its practitioners reach their full affective, physical, cognitive, and psychomotor potential.

The health and self-defense benefits of Hwa Yu T'ai Chi are unsurpassed, according to many renowned medical professionals and high-ranking black-belt martial arts instructors. The graceful, slow, spherical, flowing movements of Hwa Yu T'ai Chi increase physical and mental energy and promote a meditative, whole-mind-and-body connectedness. One cannot recognize the self-defense aspects of the art until one sees these movements sped up. Practitioners program their neuromuscular memory through slow, graceful, routine practice, to naturally and compassionately ward off, redirect, restrain, and incapacitate any harsh attack, all the while avoiding personal injury.

In this book, you will learn in full detail how Hwa Yu can aid or improve cardiovascular function and lower blood pressure; ease the effects of arthritis; and strengthen the body's structural muscles. Even moderate practice will result in less muscle and joint tension, increased energy, improved reaction time, better balance, and a more relaxed state of mind.

I have known Mr. Glenn Newth, the author of this book, both as a student and a friend, for thirty-five years. He is a dedicated, highly advanced, world-class instructor. Mr. Newth has written a book that will provide the serious student and health-care practitioner with the hidden, core principles of Hwa Yu—principles that not only illuminate this unique art, but can also be applied to every t'ai chi system in the world.

Mr. Newth's teaching of Hwa Yu is powerfully pure and astonishingly potent—combining the most advanced, practical skills for optimal health and self-defense. The reader will learn how the routine practice of this graceful healing form provides incredible benefits to all who study it. Hwa Yu T'ai Chi is a precious and rare health treasure that holds the key to living younger and experiencing an abundantly full life.

I give you my personal guarantee that this book will present you with advanced health-management skills that magnificently strengthen the muscle and skeletal systems. You will soon understand why this art is being recommended throughout the world for slowing the aging process. I hope you enjoy discovering this remarkable ancient practice.

Joyfully Your Friend—Always the Teacher, Always the Student,
Robert F. Xavier, Ph.D., Lineage Holder, Hwa Yu T'ai Chi Ch'uan
9th Degree Black Belt, Yon Ch'uan

# Introduction

This book is about an exercise that will improve your physical health, make you more relaxed and mentally alert, and improve your outlook on life from how you perceive yourself to how you view those around you. This exercise is called Hwa Yu T'ai Chi. It isn't new; it's been around for over a thousand years. It isn't costly; it can be done anywhere, and you don't need any expensive equipment to do it—just loose fitting clothes and a comfortable pair of shoes.

The reason that Hwa Yu isn't better known is that until about fifty years ago, it was a "closed-door" art, only available to a chosen few. Even in China, its place of origin, there were very few people who had ever heard of Hwa Yu. It wasn't until the 1970s that John Chung Li brought Hwa Yu to the West from Hong Kong. Today, Li's former students teach Hwa Yu throughout the U.S. and in Europe.

Most readers will be familiar with t'ai chi, and will recognize its slow, graceful, dancelike movements. As you may know, t'ai chi is a taoist system of philosophy and alchemy that combines Chi Kung (breath control) with Chinese kung fu. What makes Hwa Yu distinct from other t'ai chi forms currently taught in the West is that it follows the philosophies of the Six Combinations and Eight Methods, and the teachings of the Five-Word Song. These two critical doctrines formulate a complete system of movement education and health maintenance. By practicing and adhering to the rules explicitly defined and detailed in these two writings, it is said that a person can acquire the most sophisticated knowledge possible in regard to kinetics and body mechanics. Whereas most styles of t'ai chi have been altered after many years of being widely taught all over the world, Hwa Yu has remained pure due to its strict lineage.

It's impossible to discuss the entire philosophy and texts of Hwa Yu in one book, so I have included a specific selection of principles and exercises that will enable a person to get started on a new path to better health and personal fulfillment through Hwa Yu.

Hwa Yu is said to improve the health of those who practice it by increasing the oxygenation of muscles and internal organs, which in turn aids and increases cellular and muscular activity, providing increased energy and stamina. Hwa Yu improves muscular activity by opening up the body's motor neuron capabilities. It does this by first increasing the number of motor neurons that fire throughout the whole body during movement, and by improving and speeding up the transportation of the neural stimuli through the synapses.

Hwa Yu includes a regimen of "rooting" exercises, which are designed to teach a new student correct body and joint alignment. This alignment is crucial because it greatly improves balance and makes it possible for an individual to move with whole-body unity. Proper balance and whole-body unity allow the student to move with the least muscle resistance, adding strength, increased energy, and stamina during physical activity. This manifestation is a natural phenomenon that normally is only realized by world-class athletes and the like.

During the practice of Hwa Yu, all the muscles of the body become activated and are worked to their capacity. Whenever you move, the whole body is engaged. The spinal column is stretched throughout the exercise. The elongation of the spine also stretches the dura, which is the outer membrane surrounding the spinal cord. When the dura is stretched, the spine secretes a fluid that creates a euphoric state of mind similar to the relaxation response—the heightened state of awareness reached by practicing specific meditation techniques. This can sometimes help an individual to open the spiritual passageways that will allow him or her to find religious harmony. John Li referred to this realization as the "natural state," and said it was the ultimate goal in t'ai chi training.

In addition to numerous health benefits, training in Hwa Yu, also endows its practitioners with phenomenal skill and prowess in the area of self-defense. The combat skills embodied in Hwa Yu were developed over a thousand years ago and are among the best in the world. I studied Hwa Yu with two very talented, very different teachers: I studied extensively with John Li and then briefly with a gentlemen who simply called himself Mr. Chan. Both men were knowledgeable in various styles of kung fu, and they each knew at least three styles of t'ai chi. Both of these teachers felt that Hwa Yu was the highest form of kung fu they had ever encountered, and both felt that the self-defense skills contained within the art are unparalleled.

Many people claim that Hwa Yu is a composite of other kung fu systems. However, nothing could be further from the truth: Hwa Yu was created in 960 AD; t'ai chi ch'uan is believed to have first appeared in the late thirteenth century; Hsing I Ch'uan and Pa Kua Chang developed even later during the Ming Dynasty (placing their origins sometime in the 1500s or 1600s). This fact makes Hwa Yu one of the earliest disciplines to combine taoist breathing and meditation techniques with martial arts—thereby creating internal martial arts. Hwa Yu contains all of the philosophical and physical skills that later evolved into t'ai chi, Hsing I, and Pa Kua, which are the three most commonly practiced internal arts. Because Hwa Yu was a closed-door art that few people knew about for so long, and because it contains skills and philosophy found in the other more popular arts, people often assume that it must be a blend of these other arts—and that it must have evolved later. However, all research indicates that this presumption is incorrect.

What this all means is that because t'ai chi was created from a specific segment of Hwa Yu's teachings, they cannot be thought of as interchangeable. Hwa Yu contains all of the skills and philosophy (and health benefits) of t'ai chi, but the reverse is not always true. Hwa Yu is a complete and intricate system; t'ai chi, Hsing I, and Pa Kua, on the other hand, were created from fragments of Hwa Yu's whole, and therefore lack the full vitality of the combined teachings of the Six Combinations and Eight Methods and the Five-Word Song.

John Li, my instructor, studied Chinese martial arts his entire life. By studying the Five-Word Song and finding pieces of the puzzle from various sources, Li was able to restore the rare art of Hwa Yu to its full potency.

It is basic human nature to desire to improve one's quality of life. Hwa Yu may indeed help you improve yours. I hope you enjoy this book and realize the benefits Hwa Yu has to offer for many years to come.

# ⌁1⌁

# Hwa Yu T'ai Chi
# and Its Ancient Health Secrets

## The Beginning

For nearly one thousand years, the extraordinary secrets of Hwa Yu (pronounced "Y-U") were vigilantly guarded and only passed on from each successive master to a group of carefully chosen students. This select group generally consisted of no more than a handful of the most worthy and deserving taoist students, however, in a few rare circumstances, exceptions were made for members of either the royal family or families of other high-ranking government officials. This type of "closed-door" martial art is known as temple-style t'ai chi because it was taught only within the confines of taoist temples or retreats. Hwa Yu remained unknown to the Chinese public until the beginning of the twentieth century. At this time a few noted masters, who had been accepted into training by virtue of their social status, began to share their good fortune by offering classes in Hwa Yu to the general populace.

Although it isn't as well known as the three most common forms of internal kung fu—T'ai Chi Ch'uan, Hsing I Ch'uan, and Pa Kua Chang—Hwa Yu is a superb form of martial arts that is intricate and inclusive. T'ai Chi, Hsing I, and Pa Kua each focus on a specific aspect of Chinese metaphysics, but Hwa Yu contains the core philosophies and physical characteristics embodied within all three systems, making it more detailed and complete. Hwa Yu offers its practitioners the flowing grace of t'ai chi, the evasive nature of Pa Kua, and the powerful martial aspects of Hsing I.

Chen Hsi-I (also known as Chen Tuan), a famous taoist and Confucian scholar, invented Hwa Yu T'ai Chi in 960 AD at the beginning of the Sung Dynasty. T'ai chi first appeared in the thirteenth century, and both Hsing I and Pa Kua were developed later, sometime in the sixteenth or seventeenth centuries. This gives Hwa Yu the distinction of being one of the oldest known systems of Chinese internal kung fu (nei chia) still in existence. It also means that Hwa Yu is no mere composite of these other arts, but a pure and unique style of its own merit.

So how did Hwa Yu become accessible to the world? It is believed that Chen Hsi-I developed the art of Hwa Yu, along with several other unique forms of internal kung fu, such as T'ai Chi Ruler, while living as a recluse atop Mt. Hwa Yu in Northern China.

Chen Hsi-I originally left behind four manuscripts: Chee Hin, Ko Yung, Du Tam, and The Fable of Sam Fung. Legend goes that after Chen's death, Li Tung Fung found Chen's writings in his cave on Mt. Hwa Yu and then used them to draft the Five-Word Song. The exact origin of the Five-Word Song is somewhat sketchy: some sources say that Li's protégé, Sung Yuen Tung, is credited with its authorship. Unfortunately, Chen Hsi-I's original manuscripts are no longer known to exist. (For the full history of Hwa Yu, see Chapter 5.)

The Five-Word Song is a poem that consists of 134 lines, each containing five Chinese characters—thus the poem's name. The poem defines the principles unique to Hwa Yu. The Five-Word Song is the only written text on Hwa Yu that has been passed down to future generations. It was brought to the United States and translated into English by the late Li John Chung.

Li John Chung—or John Li, as he preferred to be called out of respect to his Christian roots—immigrated to Boston's Chinatown from Hong Kong in the early 1970s and is of direct lineage to Li Tung Fung and Chen Hsi-I. (Lineage is the progression of the art from a teacher to a student. Direct lineage means that you can trace the progression from John Li all the way back to Chen Hsi-I.) While in Boston, John Li opened a t'ai chi training center, The Hwa Yu Health Institute, to teach Americans the art of Hwa Yu as a therapeutic and restorative health-maintenance program. Mr. Li, as his students always respectfully referred to him, stated on several occasions that he had chosen to immigrate to the United States because he wanted to give something back to Americans in gratitude for their help in liberating Hong Kong from the Japanese during World War II. (Li would tell the story of how he was able to continue teaching t'ai chi classes during the occupation: the Japanese soldiers thought he was teaching dance or yoga, and therefore saw no threat in what he was doing. This amused him, since during the occupation the Japanese had curtailed or banned the practice of all forms of kung fu.)

Li brought more than sixty years of martial arts experience with him to the U.S. Although he had trained in numerous hard and soft styles, the most relevant were his training in Hwa Yu under Master Chen Yik Yan, and his Hsing I training under Master Han Xing Yuan. Under Master Han's tutelage, John Li learned three important rooting exercises: Rowing, Walking, and Standing, which he incorporated into his Hwa Yu style. (see Chapter 5.) Master Han also taught Li how to perform his movements with the correct alignment and posture so that he would remain rooted while in motion, as the Five-Word Song (FWS) requires: "When in motion, one is still rooted." (FWS, line 23)

Along with the Five-Word Song, John Li also supplied his students with the complete translation of all of the form's explanations and anecdotes that had been passed along from master to student for generations. In the years following the Sung dynasty, formal written teachings had been repressed, so teachers often used anecdotes and parables to help their students understand and retain their lessons. Li further aided his students by providing translations of the Six Combinations and Eight Methods, which are the system's fundamental rules for creating body/mind harmony, and form the philosophical basis of Hwa Yu. These principles teach us how to create internal functions from external movements. (These methods are explained in full detail in Chapter 3.)

John Li was a very charitable and giving instructor who accepted any and all students. When he opened the doors to his Boston studio, homeless people were just as welcome as the many professional and scholarly people who came to check out this new form of t'ai chi. Li believed that needy or disadvantaged people needed to learn just as much, if not more than, anyone else did, and because of this belief, never turned away any student who truly desired to learn what he was teaching.

## The Public, Family, and Temple Styles of T'ai Chi

In addition to the temple style, there are two other styles or variations of t'ai chi currently being taught throughout the world. The older and less diluted version is referred to as "family-style" t'ai chi, and the later variation is known as "public-style" t'ai chi. The main distinction of family-style t'ai chi systems is that they were handed down from father to son for generations, in order to preserve their purity. In many instances a father would decline to teach his daughters t'ai chi because they were apt to marry, which would allow the style to become randomly spread and, quite likely, skewed. Examples of family-style t'ai chi are the Yang and the Chen styles, which were kept within their respective families for hundreds of years, and have only been shared openly since the twentieth century.

Public-style t'ai chi was created in the seventeenth century, during the Ching dynasty. During this time the Manchurians had invaded and occupied China. Upon witnessing various aspects of the Chinese culture, some of the invaders developed an interest in learning the martial arts. In order to prevent the Manchurians from obtaining full knowledge of t'ai chi's fighting and health-promoting benefits, a panel of Yang Family masters configured a form in which they omitted several key physical and structural intricacies. This less potent version of the art became known as public-style t'ai chi, and is taught all around the world today. Because the movements are performed in the same graceful, slow, and flowing manner as family-style t'ai chi, it is difficult for a beginner to know if he or she is being taught an authentic form or a watered-down version. The only sure way to tell the difference between them is to practice both the family and public styles and feel the difference within one's body: while both would generate a heightened feeling of well-being, the level of intensity would vary dramatically.

In order to explain how a closed-door art (like a temple- or family-style t'ai chi) is passed on, I would like to tell the story of Dr. Lo, a good friend and one-time fellow student of John Li, my former instructor. Lo had been a serious t'ai chi student for many years, and he would practice in one of the local parks every morning and evening. One day, an elderly man approached Dr. Lo and offered to teach him a very rare form of Chi Kung called Wan Yuen. It turned out that this elderly gentleman, whose name was Lee Cheung Wah, had been visiting all the parks in the Hong Kong area for some time with the purpose of selecting two students to learn his form of Chi Kung. He did so at the urging of his son who convinced him that it was time to find someone to whom to pass his art on so that it would not go to his grave with him and be lost forever. According to the story, Master Lee was well into his nineties, and had practiced his whole life without ever teaching a single student. He chose Dr. Lo as a student because of his skill level and his dedication to t'ai chi.

Dr. Lo was so impressed with the old man that he quit his traditional medicine practice to study with his new teacher full-time. Lo's daily training consisted of three sessions; each session was three hours long and extremely grueling. Out of loyalty to his former friend, Dr. Lo sent John Li numerous films and diagrams of the Wan Yuen exercises. Li thought this training was so valuable that in his declining years he made three trips to Hong Kong in order to learn more about Wan Yuen directly from Dr. Lo. Li then passed down what he had learned from Dr. Lo to students in the United States.

## *The Name*

The complete name for Chen Hsi-I's art is Hwa Yu Hsing I Liu He Ba Fa Ch'uan. Throughout its history this art has been known by several different names, such as Dragon Boxing, Swimming or Water Boxing, and more commonly today as either Liu He Ba Fa (which literally means Six Combinations and Eight Methods) or Hwa Yu.

By adopting the name Hwa Yu, John Li utilized the segment of this long appellation that he thought was the most relevant to the art as he taught it. "Hwa Yu" as defined by Li refers to the location where the exercise was first developed, while in other contexts it symbolizes high standards in honor of its lofty place of origin. It was also Li's desire to distinguish his teachings from Liu He Ba Fa, the mainstream form of the art that was being taught throughout China and Hong Kong at the time. Li had two different teachers: Chen Yik Yang, who was more focused on the martial aspects of the art, and taught it as Liu He Ba Fa; and Fang Pak Xing, who taught more in the style of t'ai chi and was more concerned with Hwa Yu's health benefits than with its martial aspects. Li's approach to teaching the art was more in line with Master Fang's focus, so he decided to adopt a name other than Liu He Ba Fa, and decided on Hwa Yu.

It was a suggestion from his good friend and fellow t'ai chi instructor T.T. Liang (who had already built a successful following in Boston) that persuaded Li to incorporate the term t'ai chi into the name of his system, the reason being that Americans were already somewhat familiar with the term t'ai chi, but had never heard of either Liu He Ba Fa or Hwa Yu. Note that although Hwa Yu contains many of the movements and philosophies found in t'ai chi, and they are both from the same taoist roots, Hwa Yu is its own distinct art and is different than the t'ai chi that is commonly taught today.

Today, most of the active instructors in Hong Kong refer to the art as Liu He Ba Fa, while several instructors in the Shanghai and Nanking areas use the name Hwa Yu. Instructors in the United States have been known to use both names.

## The Health Benefits

The benefits of t'ai chi's slow, soft movements have been documented by several studies, such as the one sponsored by the National Institute on Aging, the results of which appeared in the May 1996 issue of the American Geriatrics Society's journal. The studies concluded that daily practice of t'ai chi is helpful in the prevention, treatment, and, often the reversal of a wide range of common disorders, such as high LDL cholesterol levels and high blood pressure. Daily t'ai chi practice strengthens the muscles, increases flexibility and bone density, and relieves cumulative emotional stress, all of which help to stave off frailty and other symptoms common with aging. People who suffer from chronic pain or tension, or loss of flexibility due to trauma, disease, or the natural aging process, can find relief as well as a new outlook on life.

Another subtle, but certainly no less important, benefit of regular t'ai chi practice is an increase in lung capacity, which improves oxygen consumption, in turn improving circulation. Increased oxygenation boosts the body's ability to remove lactic acid—a byproduct of physical exercise—from the body, and improves the efficiency of literally thousands of chemical exchanges that constantly occur within the cells of the body.

Chi is formed by a combination of breath and blood circulation. There is a second form of internal energy called *geng,* which is formed within bones, and increases as bones increase in density. When geng and chi work together, maximum benefits will be realized for both health and self-defense.

A study performed by a group of researchers in Melbourne, Australia—including Dr. Hong Xu, the coordinator of Chinese Medicine at Victoria University—compared the effects of t'ai chi, acupuncture, and herbal treatments on the symptoms of menopause and on bone loss from osteoporosis. Three separate groups were used in the study, with each using a different treatment. After a period of four months, the bone health of each participant was measured. The t'ai chi group registered the highest level of improvement in the development of healthy bone structure and increased bone density. All of the treatment methods produced significant results as far as easing the symptoms associated with menopause. (The results of the study were reported on in the February 2004 issue of *The Journal of Chinese Medicine.*)

One of the more immediate benefits of regular Hwa Yu practice is that it greatly loosens up all the joints of the body and improves their overall health. The knees, ankles, and spine will all move with ease, rather than with the stiffness and aches and pains associated with aging.

Throughout the past thirty-plus years, I have witnessed numerous occasions wherein students of Hwa Yu, including myself, were able to greatly reduce the duration of rehabilitation needed to recover from a wide range of injuries, both accidental and sports-related, by participating in daily t'ai chi practice.

In order to explain the relationship between t'ai chi and traditional Chinese medicine, Karen Borla, a licensed acupuncturist and experienced t'ai chi student told me, "Acupuncture and herbal treatments are just a part of the natural healing process. They provide a powerful shift to correct large and small imbalances in the vital energy system. However, self-care is equally, if not more, important. Preventative exercises like t'ai chi help to maintain the energy balance, so they can indeed promote better health and help prevent ailments from occurring." She continued, "Each student in my acupuncture school is required to take t'ai chi classes to learn to develop their own chi. This is very important for healthcare providers, who need strong chi and harmonious balance in order to protect their own health when dealing with many people suffering from illness. It is also important to have a first-hand experience of t'ai chi to be better able to recommend it to patients who could benefit from it." She concluded, "This first-hand experience in martial arts had a profound effect on me. I realized that t'ai chi wasn't simply an exercise, but was spiritual as well. It changed my life. I found a teacher, and I have continued to learn and practice ever since."

The principles of Hwa Yu were a revelation that enabled Chen Hsi-I to form the ultimate harmony between his mind, body, and spirit, and then combine this harmony with the martial techniques he had been taught. When utilizing these principles, new students soon find that their minds have achieved a greater level of alertness and clarity. This clarity enables their consciousness to function in the present instead of being perpetually distracted by thoughts of past or future events, a common habit that is physically exhausting and extremely draining on one's health. Living in the present has a tendency to make a person feel more vibrant and alive. From this new state of clarity and being, students can obtain a sense of lightness and harmony that can carry over into all aspects of their daily routine. This lightness and natural existence also creates a sense of ease that helps ward off disease, as it's commonly accepted that stress plays a great role in lowering the body's immune system, as well as in exacerbating existing conditions.

Lastly, practicing Hwa Yu improves the way an individual moves and carries his or her body while performing everyday tasks as well. Consequently, bone loss due to damage or natural wear-and-tear is minimized. One acquires the ability to move with the absolute least amount of muscle and or environmental resistance (the effects of gravity and other atmospheric components).

# The Wisdom

Originally, Hwa Yu was known as Water Boxing because the practitioner performed all the movements and techniques as though he or she were swimming in water—moving lightly and smoothly while being responsive and alert to what is going on around her in all directions. The power generated from these movements is continuous like a wave, and just as difficult to block or catch. While this concept may seem enigmatic, a student must fully grasp its meaning to be able to progress to advanced levels of Hwa Yu. Once this wavelike movement is achieved, the form will feel effortless and absolutely wonderful.

Hwa Yu t'ai chi incorporates specific anatomical structuring that not only makes it unprecedented, but kinesthetically superior to all other forms of internal kung fu as well. This particular structuring of the body enables students of Hwa Yu to generate all of their movements from their very core, which in turn enables them to move with what is known as "whole-body unity." The core of the body is its central axis and includes the waist, the hip joints, the base of the spine, and the tan t'ien (the center of gravity or chi). Every part of the body becomes rounded, allowing the practitioner to spiral or coil all the muscles and sinews inward and outward. This spiraling builds natural storage of kinetic energy within the body that can explode like a grenade once it is released. This energy, combined with the rounded body structure, allows a practitioner of Hwa Yu to intercept an attacker's force and instantly return it back to him at the point when he is most vulnerable. In addition, because this energy is moved through the defender's rooting and core it is greatly magnified when it is returned to the attacker.

The Five-Word Song refers to the main structural joints as "the nine joints"—two knees, two hips, two shoulders, two elbows, and the base of the spine. These nine joints all link together like a string of pearls, and enable the entire body to move as a unified whole. This structural stability, along with the improved sense of centering and balance that one acquires through practice, greatly improves one's ability and performance in other types of physical activities and sports, such as tennis, football, skiing, golf, and so on. This alignment of the structural joints—which is profoundly unique to Hwa Yu—enhances balance, and consequently enables a practitioner to expend less physical energy in performing the various movements. In other forms of t'ai chi, the pelvis is only slightly tucked and dropped and the head is raised up; this elongates the spine. In Hwa Yu, the pelvis is tucked a lot, the chest is hollowed, and the head is raised up. This gives the back a rounded appearance. In addition, in Hwa Yu, the legs are bowed out and the stance is more compact. All of this makes it easier to maintain equilibrium within the base of support, and to shift your weight from front stance to back stance. This more peripheral base of support and greater stability make Hwa Yu a very useful and practical exercise for older people, or for those individuals who are slightly disabled.

## *The Mindset of Hwa Yu*

The first three lines of the Five-Word Song instruct us to: "Empty the mind. If one thinks there is a method, that thought is in vain. With a quiet mind one can achieve harmony within as well as without and reach a natural meditative state." This mindset is essential and must be understood if you wish to be successful in learning Hwa Yu.

First, we must clear our minds of all thoughts and preconceived notions. Only then by becoming like an empty cup, we will be ready to be filled with new knowledge. Second, we must learn to be calm both in mind and body, because that is the key that enables Hwa Yu to help us develop our own vast reservoir of life-giving and health-promoting energy—the chi. When the mind is calm, a practitioner is able to harmonize with nature more freely, and as a result, perform his or her movements more fluidly and smoothly. Movement that is both fluid and smooth is an essential element for developing the ability to willfully direct the flow of chi throughout the body, otherwise known as "harnessing the chi." Chi is the basic life energy and essence that is the source of power for internal kung fu. It lies dormant in all of us until we learn to harness it through practice. Relaxation and calmness also enable a practitioner to position and maintain the major structural joints needed to properly support the body during training.

By performing the movements of Hwa Yu with a calm, clear mind, a practitioner achieves what is called the "natural state," which is the ultimate goal of Hwa Yu and most other systems of Eastern meditation. To a Christian, this means becoming one with God, while a taoist sees it as becoming "one with the ten thousand things," which is inclusive of God, nature, and the universe. No matter what philosophy or religion you follow, Hwa Yu could be the means by which you reach a higher spiritual plane.

## *Yin and Yang*

Although John Li was primarily interested in teaching Hwa Yu for its health benefits, he regularly demonstrated the form's self-defense applications to help his students better understand how to perform the movements. To understand how two opposite ends of a spectrum, such as combat and healing, meld together, we must fully understand the theory of yin and yang.

Yin and yang represent complementary opposites, such as hard and soft, light and dark, or male and female, and this balance is a key aspect of t'ai chi's essence. The theory of yin and yang more literally refers to the eternal changing of polarity. This philosophy maintains that nothing can exist as an extreme: You cannot have a situation in which something is totally hard or totally soft, nor can something be totally evil or totally good; there is a constant balancing act occurring between the two forces. For this reason, darkness always contains some degree of light, and light is offset with some degree of darkness. A male will have a certain amount of female hormones and a female will have some male hormones, while the amount or percentage of this offset will vary from one person to the next. This is why in the commonly used "two fish" yin-yang symbol, we always see some white within the black and some black within the white, with the spiral representing the ever-changing cycle of polarity.

A further example of this is found in the martial aspect of t'ai chi. If you were to block an opponent's punch with the outside of your left arm, that side of your arm becomes hard and the inside becomes soft. To balance this out, your right arm will become soft on the outside and hard on the inside, allowing you to use the inside of your right arm for a counterattack as you block.

So, when applied to t'ai chi and self-defense, the yin-yang theory implies that at all times some parts of the body are relaxed, or soft, while other parts are tense, or hard. The proportion of hardness and softness is constantly changing throughout the entire exercise. This serves to aid the chi in rising and falling within the body, which is another important principle of t'ai chi. The chi is stored within the body in an area centrally located two inches below the navel called the tan t'ien or "sea of chi." From the tan t'ien, the chi travels throughout the body via the acupuncture meridians and stimulates the various trigger points that are located along these meridians. (As a result, the practitioner's body receives health benefits equivalent to those gained from acupuncture or acupressure treatments.)

In regards to self-defense, the yin and yang, when properly applied, provide a practitioner with exceptional balance and centering, making him or her difficult, if not impossible, to knock over. By intercepting an attack with softness, a practitioner can lead an aggressor into a "void," and then counterstrike with hardness. To lead an opponent into a void is to shift the attack away from its intended target (you), either by deflecting the advance or by moving the target out of its path. With his intended target no longer obtainable, the aggressor would leave himself vulnerable to a counterattack, especially if he were to overextend his advance, thereby putting himself off-balance.

Whenever an aggressor tries to push against the body of a Hwa Yu practitioner, that portion of the practitioner's body becomes soft and absorbs the attack, drawing the aggressor into a void. The practitioner would then direct the force of the attack back to the aggressor by shifting polarity and explosively releasing the oncoming aggressive energy back to the attacker through a different channel or body part. In short, the attacker simply attacks himself. A Hwa Yu practitioner can turn almost any part of his or her body into a weapon simply by directing his or her chi into it.

The yin-yang theory is also employed in Hwa Yu's practice of rooting, which is forming a solid base of support for the body. To accomplish this, the glutei, or buttock muscles, are kept taut and tucked forward creating a pelvic tilt; the large muscles in the legs become naturally firm from their effort to support the body's weight. Line forty-seven of the Five-Word Song states, "Distribution of weight between one leg and another is clearly distinguished." This means that the percentage of total body weight that either leg supports throughout the exercise is in a constant state of change, adhering to the principles of yin-yang. Below the tan t'ien the body is firm and heavy like the earth, while above the tan t'ien the body is light, emulating the sky. Lines forty-eight and forty-nine provide us with the information that supports these theories by stating, "The body is of both yin and yang, empty and solid; and by emptying oneself the opponent's force is led to a void." One last line relevant to this topic is, "Your footing should be forty percent to the front and sixty percent to the rear," (FWS, line 59) or vice versa in accordance with yin and yang. If a practitioner were to commit more than sixty percent of his or her body weight either forward or backward, it would become proportionally more difficult to maintain the center of gravity, which in turn would leave him or her increasingly vulnerable to attack.

The yin-yang theory is so well employed in Hwa Yu that the instant an attacker makes contact, every segment of the practitioner's body springs into action to correct the imbalance and turn the attack around.

Grand Master John Chung Li in a posture from Streams
Flow Incessantly.

# ~2~

# The Structure of Hwa Yu T'ai Chi

## Overview

Hwa Yu, as taught by John Li, is the perfect harmony of t'ai chi, Hsing I, and Pa Kua techniques. Although some instructors emphasize one form over the others, Li expounded the finer points of all three equally. Pa Kua is an evasive style, and it's the most practical one for smaller individuals. It's also very useful in situations that simply require warding off an aggressor who is being more of a nuisance than a real threat; for example, these techniques are practical for law-enforcement officers when they need to restrain a suspect without inflicting excessive physical harm. Hsing I is very direct in its approach, perfect for quickly defusing attacks before they have a chance to get started (i.e., attacking the attack). If any skills have been altered from their original forms as practiced in T'ai Chi, Hsing I, or Pa Kua, this has occurred solely for the purpose of giving practitioners greater control of their opponents. Any differences between the techniques used in Hwa Yu and those found in its sister arts are, like most everything else in the Hwa Yu repertoire, very subtle and difficult to detect without a highly trained eye.

Control over opponents is an important concept to Hwa Yu; all movements are formulated to constantly shift the advantage in a confrontation back to the Hwa Yu practitioner. All strikes are targeted either to vital areas of the attacker's body, such as the eyes, the throat, the sternum, or the groin, or to various *dim mak* points (vulnerable spots located along the acupuncture meridians). The coiling of various muscles, learned throughout the forms, plays an important role in delivering these blows.

Hwa Yu employs movements that are shorter and more compact than other t'ai chi systems. These compact movements give Hwa Yu its smooth graceful appearance. This smoothness calms the nervous system, and helps develop superior balance and coordination in its practitioners. By using shorter movements, the practitioner always keeps his or her hands in close proximity to each other, providing a potential adversary with fewer opportunities to penetrate his or her defenses. This protective posture is usually referred to as "closing the gates." One advantage of keeping such a closed guarded position at all times is that while one hand blocks an oncoming attack, the other hand is already in position to counterstrike the opponent either simultaneously or immediately after the block. One last benefit of keeping the hands close together is that if one arm is needed to support or aid the other—as in the case of an augment block—it can to do so quite easily.

Hwa Yu is an effective means of self-defense for practitioners of all shapes and sizes, because it enables its exponents to absorb any force and to maintain their equilibrium while doing so. This makes it possible for a smaller person to fend off an attacker of greater size. In addition, Hwa Yu practitioners have a variety of options when forced to deal with a physical confrontation. For example, when defusing attacks that are not life threatening, evasive or restraining techniques can be utilized in order to minimize any harm inflicted upon the aggressors. However, in the event that a practitioner is assaulted with a very strong or life-threatening attack, Hwa Yu equips its practitioners to respond in kind and with far more devastating results. The decision of whether to attack or to simply protect oneself, and of how much force to use when doing so, often must be made in an instant. For this reason, meditation and mental conditioning are a vital part of the training process. The verses from the Five-Word Song that relate to this principle are: "Although the opponent is busy, one should stays calm when awaiting him." (FWS, line 28); and "Be calm as a resting Buddhist." (FWS, line 39)

## Getting Started

Hwa Yu, like all systems of martial arts, is a format of techniques and skills patterned specifically to teach potential students the fundamental concepts and movements associated with combat. These skills are arranged in a specific order starting with the most elementary and progressing in a logical manner to those that are more intricate and refined.

John Li believed that rooting is the first skill a beginner needed to learn; according to him, students were wasting their time if they started learning the forms without first mastering the three rooting exercises. These exercises strengthen the leg muscles, enabling a student to practice for longer periods of time. Increasing leg strength also helps to alleviate excess muscular tension, thereby expediting the student's progress in developing chi. Most t'ai chi systems teach that it is vital to practice some sort of strength training—like these rooting exercises—early on because it will precipitate one's ability to develop the correct body structure, which in turn enables him or her to better circulate his or her chi.

All new students begin their training with the first two rooting exercises: Rowing and Walking. In ancient times, a beginner would spend an entire year practicing only these two exercises, but John Li was a bit more lenient—he would only require that a new student spend four to six weeks Rowing and Walking before he allowed them to move on. After achieving some degree of competency in these first two exercises, students are then ready to learn the third rooting exercise, Standing, which is by far the most difficult of the three main rooting exercises. (see Chapter 5 for detailed explanations of the rooting exercises.)

Once a student has learned to root him or herself, he or she is then ready to move on to the next phase of Hwa Yu and begin learning the forms. The first set of Hwa Yu forms is called the Twelve Animal Set, which is a series of twelve short forms, each consisting of roughly five or six movements that mimic different animals. The twelve animals imitated in this set are: the bear, the crane, the tiger, the snake, the pang (a mythical Chinese bird), the leopard, the unicorn, the eagle, the goose, the falcon, the dragon, and the ape. All of these short forms can be linked together in various combinations to make several medium-length forms or a single complete practice routine. The Animal Forms contain a lot of self-defense applications, but their most important function is to teach new students how to transfer external movement into an internal activity.

The Animal Forms are made up of basic Hwa Yu movements that prepare a student for the more advanced and intricate movements that embody the main Hwa Yu form, known as the long form. This form consists of 384 movements, each with numerous self-defense applications. (This number correlates to the total combination of lines in the I Ching.) Hwa Yu's long form is divided into two halves, with each serving a specific purpose. The first half, which is the longer of the two, should be practiced in the style of t'ai chi—slow, even, and smooth, like floating on air. The reason for doing it in this manner is to increase the circulation and flow of chi throughout the body and to obtain an understanding of the inner workings of the art. In the second half, the student learns how to perform the movements with the spirit of the dragon, the snake, and the monkey. Each of these methods conveys life to the form, giving it an attitude and feeling all its own, while providing the practitioner with the chance to express and exercise the storage of chi that he has developed from practicing the first half. The dragon uses a lot of vertical motion, which enables the student to use his or her natural body strength (provided by the main structural joints and their corresponding muscles) to easily unbalance or strike an attacker. The snake is twisty and clever, constantly moving to one side and then attacking the other. Lastly, the monkey is nimble and quick, with movements that are shorter and more abrupt than the other variations.

The first five sections of the long form are presented in later chapters. I focused on these because they contain movement skills that must be mastered, and that can't readily be learned from other techniques. The moves in the first five sections will instill basic internal concepts and centering skills, and will help train you to sit into your hip flexors for better balance control.

After learning the long form, students can further develop and advance their techniques by practicing a two-person exercise called Push Hands, which is the practical or combat form of t'ai chi training. For this training you must first find a good partner, then proceed by moving slowly and softly, in the style of t'ai chi. Once the basic concepts have been mastered, the exercise can be done faster. The object of Push Hands is to uproot or strike your partner (if you can), by using skills that you have cultivated from the forms. (Please note that it is never necessary to strike your partner with full-power blows during Push Hands. For the purpose of training, a simple light tap will help show your partner his or her mistake.) By practicing with partners, students develop sensitivity, learning how to feel an attacker's energy and absorb or immobilize this energy. It isn't necessary to know the entire long form in order to begin practicing Push Hands; students who only know part of the form can hone their skills and benefit from this training as well.

The practice of Push Hands is intended to be a learning experience, not a test of one's superiority over other students. However, tournaments for Push Hands are held all around the world today, and if these events are held in the spirit of sportsmanship and fellowship, they can be a very educational experience.

# Body Position

As it is with nature, all the movements in t'ai chi follow a circular pattern, with the practitioner moving his body as if he were standing in a giant sphere and all of his motions must conform to the inner surface of this sphere. In Hwa Yu, a student is taught to maintain roundness in all areas of her body: The arms are kept round, as if she were hugging someone; the legs are bowed outward to create peripheral stability in her stance; and the feet grip the ground, activating the arches and aiding balance. The tailbone and the buttocks muscles tilt forward, and the chest hollows. This will give the back a rounded appearance; however, the body's alignment remains erect because the hips and shoulders are located along the same vertical plane. This positioning of the body is referred to as "straight but not straight," and "bent but not bent." The tucking of the buttocks and pelvis creates what is known as the "pelvic bowl." When you have tucked your pelvis into this position it aligns the organs within the abdomen so that they naturally support each another.

Even the hands and tongue are held in rounded positions while practicing. The tongue is curled back against the roof of the mouth, as this position creates saliva that helps cool the throat and stave off thirst during practice. Also, when it is kept in this position, the tongue acts as a buffer to prevent the teeth from banging together. The hands and fingers are curved both length- and widthwise (the thumb drops down slightly creating a curve much like the arch of a foot), with the thumb and index finger forming an arch called the Tiger's Mouth. This helps draw the chi through the hands, which are one of the five main terminals, and is also useful for many self-defense applications. All of these curves open the body's channels and allow the chi to flow freely. The bowed legs and arched feet enhance balance by enabling the practitioner to plant the outside edges of the feet solidly onto the ground. This allows the practitioner to use the entire surface area of the foot to support the body or to push off from when advancing or retreating, and it also creates peripheral stability to his stance. Even though it is extremely important, this type of stability is almost never found in other martial arts systems.

Lastly, a student should activate the five terminals (the two feet, the two hands, and the crown of the head) and stretch his neck by pulling it upward from the nape. Doing so, while tucking your chin, will force your head to rise up. Rising up the head lifts the spirits and causes the chi to rise upward and elevate your alertness and level of clarity—you will feel totally alive and in harmony with the world. The practice of

Hwa Yu should leave an individual feeling fully energized and euphoric. With continued practice, this euphoric state will begin to be a part of the student's everyday life. Those individuals who are prone to outbursts of temper will become more patient and tolerant, while those who are overly withdrawn and self-reflective will become more social. This newfound state of relaxation should give the student of Hwa Yu increased composure and an air of self-confidence that will forever change his or her life for the better. Once a student has become centered and balanced, his movements will then be more natural, which in turn will allow him to move in a manner that places minimal stress on his joints (especially the knees, spine, and neck). This is helpful in reducing or eliminating common back or neck pain, and will keep the bones and joints healthy as one reaches old age.

## Levels and Ranking

Although Hwa Yu does not employ a belt-ranking system like those used in such martial arts as judo or karate, there are four levels of proficiency in Hwa Yu. First-level students perform the movements entirely with their muscles. Experiencing pain and stiffness at this level is common as the skeletal muscles become overworked; at first, there is a great deal of tension in all of the muscles, which causes them to fight against one another, impeding a student's movements and, consequently, the circulation of his or her chi. So, the first level is about overcoming this discomfort and strengthening the muscles.

The second level is often referred to as the bone level. This means that the internal structure of one's stance has been perfected, and one's bone density and strength have greatly improved. When a student has reached this stage of training, the energy for her movements is derived from the bones and the deep-muscle tissue. The muscles become looser and more relaxed, and the student's body weight sinks down into his root and tan t'ien. The student's movements become effortless, and her form starts to appear very graceful, as if she were moving through water. With the skeletal structure carrying the bulk of the body weight, the muscles will relax, and the blocks or hindrances will cease to exist. This causes the movements to look livelier, as though the student is imbued with the essence of a snake or a dragon.

Level three is sometimes called the chi level. When a student reaches this level, it's the circulation of his chi radiating upward from his tan t'ien that propels his movements. The core of the body (hips and spine) is the axis through which this energy emanates. The final or fourth level (which has no easy nickname) is reached when the movements and the chi are both energized and controlled entirely by the spirit. Level one denotes a beginning student; level two signifies an advanced student. A practitioner who has reached level three is considered to be a master, while level four typifies a senior- or high-level master. Very few practitioners ever attain the fourth level.

Hwa Yu, as with most other internal kung fu systems, is a lifelong endeavor. These arts are so deep that it takes many years to reach the level of master. And no matter how many years—or decades—a student practices this art, new things will continue to reveal themselves to him or her. For instance, something a teacher says during training one day may not seem very important at the time, but then five years later while practicing, something clicks and the student realizes, "Oh, that's what he meant." The Five-Word Song states, "All progress toward the truth of this exercise is very delicate," but "if one's mind is made up to learn, there will be success." (FWS, lines 75 & 85)

## The Value of the Five-Word Song

One of the final lines in the Five-Word Song reads, "For those who set out to find the truth to this exercise, do not misjudge the value of the Five-Word Song." I have provided verses from the Five-Word Song throughout this book with the hope that they will help readers assimilate the essence of Hwa Yu. The entire Five-Word Song, originally translated by John Li, can be found in Chapter Three. It was Li's belief that many of the modern Hwa Yu instructors had seriously strayed away from these important teachings, and their art suffered for it.

In several instances Li Tung Fung, the author of the Five-Word Song, used more than one verse to discuss a single topic, in order to emphasize its importance. As we noted earlier, being calm in the face of an attack is one topic that is often expounded upon; the importance of daily practice is another.

## Internal vs. External Styles

In contrast to external kung fu styles, which are dynamic, internal forms are always practiced slowly, calmly, and evenly. While chi and flexibility are the source of strength in internal styles, external styles derive their power more from muscle and sinew conditioning. For example, in an external kung fu style, a student undergoes a rigorous exercise routine to develop the fundamental attributes of physical fitness: strength, stamina, flexibility, endurance, motor coordination, and aerobic capacity. Students learn to defend against attacks by using their strength and conditioning in conjunction with techniques that employ these abilities most effectively in accordance with the basic laws of physics and body mechanics. By contrast, an internal stylist learns to move the inner atmosphere around the body by employing specific breathing and visualization techniques, while performing slow, fluid, and relaxed movements. By relaxing the muscles and sinews the practitioner opens up the arteries and blood vessels, the result of which is enhanced circulation and chi flow. It all appears to be an elegant dance, however, it is extremely powerful in its resolve. John Li would often state, "It's natural," when referring to t'ai chi, because it follows the philosophy of the Tao. Other types of martial arts encompass different philosophies as their core; for example, most modern karate systems adhere to Japanese Bushido, and there are a select few forms of karate that embrace Zen philosophy.

In the practice of Hwa Yu, the mind forms the idea of the movement and then projects that idea forth, expressing it outward and directing the chi and spirit to flow along with the movement. All of this requires a structured mental process that resembles a sophisticated system of meditation, the result of which is very calming and rewarding, psychologically and emotionally. Because of this, children are not usually ready for this type of training, and therefore, usually gain more from practicing an external style. It should be noted that while external styles are less focused on internal meditation, they still offer a great deal of mental conditioning that can prepare a young student for a more philosophical system, such as Hwa Yu, in the future. External stylists must learn to focus their full attention on the movements or techniques they are performing in exclusion of all other thoughts. This not only serves to help them improve their techniques, but also helps them learn to focus in the face of an attack. While internal systems employ several types of meditation all at once, external systems use a basic form, which is called "concentrated meditation." A good external style instructor will often introduce his students to more complex types of meditation as they progress in their training and improve their ability to concentrate.

For those students looking for quick results, the external arts provide a more immediate understanding in the area of self-defense. After just a few short months of practicing, an external stylist could have the ability to defend him- or herself against most unskilled attackers. In many cases, potential muggers carefully choose victims who appear weaker than them, because although they may be tough, most muggers are not highly skilled fighters. These aggressors simply rely on a few specific techniques that have brought them prior success. On the other hand, should a confrontation occur involving two trained individuals, the outcome is usually determined by who has trained the most and the hardest. Only when these factors are somewhat equal does the type of training that each underwent become critical

Although the internal arts take longer to master and produce results in the area of combat, there is a sister art to Hwa Yu called Yon Ch'uan (Soft Fist) that is specifically fashioned to arm a student with solid self-defense skills in a relatively short period of time. It employs skills that are found in various martial arts, such as judo, karate, aikido, and kung fu, as well as Hwa Yu, and incorporates the principles of the Six Combinations and Eight Methods. This synthesis forms an art that is both hard and soft, or part external and part internal. The reason for using techniques from numerous martial arts is to provide a practitioner with as many options as possible. For example, aikido or judo skills can be utilized in situations that do not require extreme or deadly force, such as subduing a party guest who had too much to drink. On the other hand, karate or jiujitsu skills can be applied on those rare occasions when there is no alternative but to use extreme force to subdue a vicious attacker. Another advantage to having a wide range of skills is that certain types of martial arts such as jiujitsu, judo, and aikido are more aptly suited for close-range attacks (when an attacker has his hands on you, as in the case of a chokehold or collar grab), while arts such as karate or tae kwon do are better suited for defending oneself against long-range attacks (when an attacker is positioned outside of your reach and is in the process of moving in closer in order to deliver a punch or kick). Yon Ch'uan is a practical self-defense art, but a potential student must be willing and able to undergo the rigorous training that the external styles demand.

In the long run, the internal styles provide a superb form of self-defense. But because of the very complex physical movements and mental practices the internal arts employ, students must practice them diligently for a considerable period of time before they are able to apply these skills effectively in actual self-defense situations. Each individual's success in this area will be determined by how often and how intensely he or she practices. While some students could realize this ability in a year or so, others could need four or five years before their techniques are effective in combat. The Five-Word Song states, "If one does not practice regularly, then do not face the enemy." (FWS, line 22) Another verse assures us that with practice, "deeper progress can be made: from the door to the hall to the temple with one's master." (FWS, line 70)

Karen Borla and I demonstrate "Heavenly Rulers Point to the Sky."

# 3

## The Six Combinations and Eight Methods & The Five-Word Song

The Six Combinations and Eight Methods are the pivotal philosophies and principles that constitute Hwa Yu and also distinguish it from all other types of t'ai chi and internal martial arts. It is vitally important that new students study these principles and their significance before learning the art. The Five-Word Song states, "If one wishes to learn this internal exercise, then one must first learn the Eight Methods." (FWS, line 11)

As noted in Chapter One, "Six Combinations and Eight Methods" is the literal English translation of Liu He Ba Fa, which is why this particular name is often used to denote this amazing internal martial art. (In some instances, this name is simplified to Six and Eight). The Six Combinations (Liu He) will be discussed first because they provide new students with the important steps for creating mind, body, and spiritual unity and for learning to harmonize with nature and one's environment. We will then learn about the Eight Methods (Ba Fa), which are the fundamental rules or guidelines necessary for the correct performance of the Hwa Yu forms.

The Six Combinations and Eight Methods should be studied often in the beginning, and then revisited from time to time as one becomes more advanced in the study of Hwa Yu. A new and deeper understanding of these texts will be had with each new reading regardless of how many years a person studies this immensely detailed holistic art. Because of this aspect, the art and its principles can be compared to a very deep well, in that no matter how much water (or information) you draw from it, there is still far more left in the well.

Please note that the information on the Six Combinations and Eight Methods in this chapter was transcribed from original notes given to me by John Li. Some of the information has been paraphrased for greater clarity.

# The Six Combinations (Liu He)

1. The body combines with the mind.

The mind must first be calm, as stated in the opening line of the Five-Word Song; then it directs the body to move. When the body is relaxed and held in the correct posture, it will be ready to follow whatever directions the mind initiates. This combination of events enables the body and mind to function harmoniously, which will eliminate any hesitation in the practitioner's response to attacks. Remember: the body and mind will only become truly united when the mind is calm and the body relaxed.

2. The mind combines with the idea.

The mind first forms an idea of what to do, or how to respond to a given stimulus, and then directs the body to react. The mind starts the process and supplies the initiating or driving force to the body. Moving one's body or reacting without first forming an idea would create an empty response. In self-defense situations it is important that we first empty our mind, and then watch intently for the enemy's weak spots. Once this weakness reveals itself, your mind immediately makes a decision, and you launch your attack quickly.

3. The idea combines with the chi.

Once you have an idea of what to do, you direct and circulate your chi. Coordinating your breath with the movement will cause the chi to become concentrated and it too will flow along with the movement. Remember that chi is developed only with daily practice; without regular practice the chi flow will be minimal, and difficult to feel or coordinate with your movement.

4. The chi combines with the spirit.

Once you are able to get your chi to rise with the movements, you can learn to let the chi direct the movement by itself. The next step is to let both the chi and the spirit (or will) drive and control the movement. When this is accomplished all movements will look lively and elegant, displaying both grace and finesse, because you are now moving with your internal energy.

5. The spirit combines with the movement.

Putting your spirit into the movements will make them lively, like a dragon at play. Without this spirit in them, the movements would appear stilted and dull. The waist is the axis that initiates these movements, and your will directs the spirit.

6. The movement combines with the air.

The Five-Word Song tells us to move like "a fairy dancing in the clouds." (FWS, line 62) The Hwa Yu practitioner should move as if he or she were floating on air, or as if he or she were a fish swimming through water. Only when you are able to move as if you are floating lightly on air, and synchronize all of your body parts into whole-body unity, will you be able to attain the highest goal of this exercise, which is the natural state of being. To reach this advanced level, total relaxation of one's body must be achieved, so that a lot of the physical work is performed by deep-muscle tissue. This realization is difficult for a beginner to grasp, but once he/she achieves this feeling, he/she should always follow this principle during practice.

# The Eight Methods (Ba Fa)

While the Six Combinations provide us with the information necessary to move in harmony with ourselves and with nature, the Eight Methods contain the components that enable us to apply internal concepts to exterior movement—and move with full body unity. The Eight Methods are the more practical side of Hwa Yu and can be applied directly to combat or self-defense.

1. Chi: The chi works internally, concentrated by one's spirit.

The chi (internal life energy) regulates the flow of the blood as it circulates throughout the body. Our spirit is what expresses and regulates movement, up and down, left and right, and so on. When the spirit is activated it enables us to concentrate our full attention on the movements as we perform them. The spirit of the movement is shown through the eyes of the Hwa Yu practitioner as he or she executes the various forms. When a practitioner moves like a tiger, the energy and expression of a tiger will show in his or her eyes. The spirit helps the movement of the chi, which in turn creates lively movements. Chi without spirit in it is very dull. Remember the chi emanates throughout the body from the tan t'ien, or sea of chi. The tan t'ien is the well from which all energy and movement springs forth. The chi lies dormant in everybody until it is activated by regular and continued t'ai chi practice. In the advanced stage of training, we combine the spirit and the chi and direct this powerful entity with our mind. This practice makes our movements gratifying. As the Five-Word Song notes, "the internal force [chi and geng] is wonderfully rewarding." (FWS, line 42)

2. Bone: The internal force is concealed.

There is another form of internal force called *geng,* which is concealed within the bones and joints of the body until it is needed or awakened by practice. Geng is an entity that cannot be expressed in words; when it is needed, it springs forth suddenly, and then just as quickly subsides. This allows the Hwa Yu player to change from soft (yin) to hard (yang) without the opponent detecting a change in the feeling of the motion from passive to aggressive. The internal force is more powerful if we root ourselves and push from the rear leg. As noted earlier, if we practice our rooting from the beginning, our internal training will be stronger later on. Learning to maintain the correct roundness of posture and proper joint alignment will aid the movement and intensity of the geng. By developing the ability to raise and lower one's chi the Hwa Yu student attains the ability to compress the chi within the tan t'ien, which in turn moves the energy into the bones to form geng. This internal energy spirals, and is willed and directed by the mind.

3. Feature: Movement is fluid and continuous.

When we start to learn the movements of Hwa Yu, we must try to perform each movement as perfectly as we can by fully expressing every detail. It is important during this time to make each movement precise so that we achieve a clear understanding of all the movements and their functions. John Li would tell us, "Practice until you can do it perfectly." After we have learned to execute each movement correctly, we can then move to a more advanced stage of training wherein the movements all blend together into a continuous series of smooth, fluid circles. At this level, all of the form's movements seem to have become one, without interruption from beginning to end.

4. Follow: Meet an opponent's force with circular movement, interpreting the force and yielding to it.

The best medium for learning the principle of follow is the practice of Push Hands. In this exercise we train our senses by relaxing our body and maintaining a very light touch with our partner, enabling us to follow and interpret his or her every movement. By lightly sticking to our opponent we will be able to feel his or her oncoming force and either yield to it, or redirect it. (In Push Hands it's necessary to maintain contact with your partner/opponent at all times; this contact is generally on the lower forearms or hands, but shifts as is appropriate). When our touch is light we can easily read our opponent's intentions. On the other hand, if we try to anticipate the attack mentally, we will fail to feel it and quite likely end up being hit by it. Also, by maintaining a light touch we will be able to follow our opponent's retreat and counterattack him or her. This principle is called "stick and follow." The opponent will have a difficult time knowing where your attack is coming from because your touch is so light. As you get more advanced in your internal arts training, you will be able to feel your opponent's chi as he or she advances toward you. The stronger this ability becomes, the lighter your touch can be. A lighter touch means greater relaxation and, therefore, greater understanding.

5. Rise: One's head is held as if suspended from above, and relaxed.

The principles of t'ai chi are in accordance with those of the I Ching. The I Ching is composed of 64 hexagrams—a hexagram is composed of six lines that represent either yin or yang. There are two trigrams that compose a given hexagram, and each trigram has three lines. The top line of the trigram is heaven, the bottom is earth, and the middle line is man. It is necessary for man to maintain his balance between heaven and earth. While doing t'ai chi or Hwa Yu, your head emulates the top line and stretches up lightly as if it were floating in heaven. (Always stretch upward from the tan t'ien to the crown of the head.) This lightness will enable the chi to move from the base of the spine upward to the back of the head, then to recede back down the front of the body back to the tan t'ien. This is like a river returning to the sea. The chi rising and circulating in this manner will enable the mind to become alert and clear, and it will help the body to move with balance and harmony.

6. Return: To maintain an even balance, movement in one direction is tied to its opposite (to and fro, up and down, left and right, in and out).

The principle of return involves the balance between substantial and insubstantial, or yin and yang. More simply stated, it is the means of maintaining perfect balance while advancing or retreating. As we previously learned, our legs should be bowed, and our backs and arms should be rounded. All movement, forward or backward (advancing or retreating), is controlled by the waist and the spine. It is awkward to achieve this balance at first, but to-and-fro movement is the best tool for teaching us to move in accordance with yin and yang, and Rowing is the perfect exercise for practicing this principle. (see Chapter 5.)

We must remember that all movement is generated from and spirals around the body from the tan t'ien. This, according to the principle of return, means that if any body part is moving forward then another or a corresponding part must be moving backward. The centrifugal force of moving away from the center is accelerated through the centripetal force of return: all parts maintain a perfect harmony and balance while the body is in motion. Many highly trained and accomplished athletes experience this powerful harmony, and are able to perform with a natural sense of ease. This acceleration of intrinsic energy is nearly impossible to teach others; they all must learn it for themselves. The relationship of yin and yang is the guide. The term t'ai chi means extreme ultimate, and when we employ the return principle we are referring to extreme ultimate balance.

7. Restrain: The mind should be calm, maintaining an inner void.

The principle of restraint (meaning to keep in check) is paramount to maintaining a calm mind in the midst of a tense situation: "Although the opponent is busy, you should remain calm when awaiting him," (FWS, line 28). Calmly watch the enemy, while maintaining an inner void. From this calmness will arise the idea of how to meet the attack at the instant the assailant enters your reach.

8. Conceal: The inner force is concealed until it is needed.

With enough practice you will reach an advanced skill level in Hwa Yu, and once this has been achieved, you will have acquired a strong inner force that is stored within your bones. Although you would be aware of its presence, it is intangible and, therefore, would lie hidden from any would-be attackers. If an attack should occur, then you would release the inner force suddenly, and with complete surprise to the attacker. Often, people that I meet for the first time will say to me, "Gee, you don't look like a tough martial artist!" This is a complement as far as I am concerned, because I know that I am concealed. I don't walk around with a puffed-up macho attitude, but on the contrary, appear almost meek and mild. However, my strength is on the inside, and, as such, it is controlled by my spirit and chi.

A practitioner also learns to conceal all vital self-defense applications during practice. The highest form of Hwa Yu is to practice without this intent in order to achieve total relaxation and harmony. Remember the beginning: empty the mind.

# The Five-Word Song  (又 稱 心意功)

1. Empty your mind.

   心 意 本 無 法

2. If you think there is a method, that thought is in vain.

   有 法 是 虛 無

3. In making the mind void of thought, one can achieve a natural meditative state.

   虛 無 得 自 然

4. With a calm mind one is free from hesitation.

   無 法 不 容 怨

5. A quiet mind opens the passageway to harmony within, as well as without.

   放 之 弥 六 合

6. Fill the sky and the earth within, as well as without.

   包 羅 小 天 地

7. This relates to the Buddhist's idea that is conveyed by the circle.

   釋 家 為 圓 覺

8. The Taoists say it is not one's will, but the will of nature.

   道 家 說 無 為

9. In the beginning, while doing the exercise, one reveals each feature of the movement. But with practice these features flow into one.

   有 象 求 無 象

10. This fluidness of movement cannot be anticipated—it develops naturally through practice.

    不 期 自 然 至

11. & 12. If one wishes to learn this internal exercise, you must first learn the Eight Methods.

要學心意功　先從八法起

13. Practicing this exercise maintains one's broadminded spirit.

養我浩然氣

14. The entire body becomes elastic (springlike).

遍身皆彈力

15. The beginning of the internal force can be recognized by the opponent—but not its end.

見首不見尾

16. When the exercise is mastered, one's feature and intent are unrecognizable.

無象亦無意

17. Movement to and fro (back and forward) is not revealed.

收放勿露形

18. The relaxing and flexing of movement is self-determined.

鬆緊要自主

19. One must face an attack with calmness.

策應宜守默

20. The body should be straight in stance.

不偏亦不倚

21. Although the opponent sees no resistance in your stance, this is false because you are concealed.

視不能而能

22. If one does not practice regularly, then do not face the enemy.

生疏莫臨敵

23. When in motion, one is still rooted.

動 時 把 得 固

24. Do not overextend yourself to the opponent.

一 發 未 深 入

25. Judge the chance and take the opportunity.

審 機 得 其 勢

26. One strikes with internal force before the opponent can advance with strength.

乘 勞 毫 与 顧

27. When the opponent is hard, then one is soft.

剛 在 他 力 前

28. & 29. Although the opponent is busy, one should stay calm when awaiting him.

柔 乘 他 力 後 　 彼 忙 我 靜 待

30. Whether to attack or to protect is according to one's own decision.

攻 守 任 君 鬥

31. Take the first opportunity and be quicker than the opponent.

步 步 占 先 機

32. Always concentrate on the situation.

時 時 要 留 意

33. Conceal one's force like the bow: round and ready to spring.

蓄 力 如 弓 圓

34. Attack as an arrow: quick and straight.

發 勁 似 箭 直

35. One should thoroughly understand the principle of yin and yang.

悟 透 陰 陽 理

36. Both yin and yang flow in and out, are hard and soft, and are of mutual use.

剛 柔 互 為 就

37. Breathing is regular from the bottom of the abdomen to the heart.

調 息 坎 離 交

38. This cyclic up-and-down breathing smoothes the chi.

上 下 中 和 氣

39. Be calm as a resting Buddhist.

守 默 如 卧 禪

40. Move like a dragon rising from hibernation.

勁 似 蟄 龍 起

41. This calmness appears empty, but it is not—there is something within.

虛 靈 含 有 物

42. The internal force is wonderfully rewarding.

窈 窈 溟 溟 趣

43. The internal force can be suddenly concealed or suddenly expressed.

忽 隱 又 忽 現

44. All breathing shall be natural.

息 息 任 自 然

45. Yield to heavy attack.

避 免 敵 重 力

46. Every action is self-initiated.

原 來 自 我 始

47. The distribution of weight between one leg and another is clearly distinguished.

双 单 可 分 明

48. The body is of both yin and yang; it is both empty and solid.

陰 陽 見 虛 实

49. By emptying oneself, the opponent's force is led to a void.

虛 引 敵 落 空

50. If the enemy should retreat, stick with a quick advance.

欲 收 放 更 急

51. The legs should be curved like a bow.

兩 腿 似 弓 彎

52. When advancing or retreating use force derived from the kidneys.

伸 縮 腰 着 力

53. The arms and back should be round as if hugging.

臂 脊 須 圓 抱

54. Circulate your chi from the inside to the outside.

内 外 混 元 氣

55. & 56. Stop trivial thoughts and concentrate on your movement as if you were facing a difficult enemy.

息 念 要 集 神   彷 彿 臨 大 敵

57. Your eyes move about like lightening.

目 光 如 流 電

58. Your spirit watches in all four directions (front, back, left, and right).

猪 神 顧 四 隅

59. Your footing should be forty percent to the front and sixty percent to the rear.

前 四 後 佔 六

60. The hands are thirty percent to the front and seventy percent to the rear.

拿 揑 三 分 七

61. & 62. The feature of the movement is like swimming in water.

若 履 雲 霧　形 動 如 洺 水

63. The movement is light, like a fairy dancing in the clouds.

飄 飄 乎 欲 仙

64. The idea is very great, but there is nothing; it is like the great void.

浩 浩 乎 清 虛

65. The idea of the movement is like a fierce tiger.

意 動 似 慄 虎

66. The calmness of the chi is very gentle.

氣 靜 如 處 子

67. Once the enemy is offensive, he is defeated.

犯 者 敵 郎 仆

68. The inner strength controls the five terminals and the nine joints.

五 綜 九 節 力

69. If one wishes to learn, one must practice frequently.

欲 學 持 有 恒

70. In this way, deeper progress can be made: from the door to the hall to the temple with one's master.

升 堂 可 入 室

71. When the exercise is mastered, one's inner force can be concealed or expressed at will.

顯 隱 無 so 有

72. Focus your spirit to discover the truth.

凝 神 尋 真 諦

73. This harmonious exercise combines all movement.

妙 法 有 和 合

74. The quiet and emptiness of this exercise separates one from worldly things.

離 塵 空 虛 寂

75. & 76. Remember that all progress toward the truth of this exercise is very delicate.

拳 拳 得 服 膺　　道 理 極 微 細

77. The idea of the movement is to seem not to move, achieving fluidness.

欲 動 似 非 動

78. One's calmness combines with the idea.

靜 中 遠 有 意

79. Cease all thoughts and your chi will become calm naturally.

息 念 氣 自 平

80. Quietly maintain the "Great Emptiness."

默 默 守 太 虛

81. One's basic foundation is built through this exercise.

元 根 筑 基 法

82. In this exercise all valuable points are concealed.

蘊 藏 皆 珠 玉

83. If you ask, "Is it hard to learn?" The answer is "No, it is not."

說 难 、亦 不 難

84. It looks easy at first, but no, it is not easy.

看 易 本 非 易

85. If one's mind is made up to learn, there will be success.

有 志 事 竟 成

86. In this world there is nothing of real difficulty.

世 間 無 難 事

87. To learn, one must be sincere and determined.

欲 學 果 有 誠

88. This depends on long and frequent practice, and wisdom.

久 恒 与 智 慧

89. This exercise was invented by Chen Hsi-I of Hwa Yu.

華 嶽 希 夷 門

90. The student of Hwa Yu should practice every day; this is most important.

力 行 最 為 貴

91. There must be concentration of the spirit and the idea.

神 意 要 集 中

92. All the joints of the body move together.

推 動 靜 轉 器

93. When contact is made, the inner force comes forth at once.

一 觸 力 即 蓄

94. This gives no opportunity for the opponent to escape.

推 動 靜 轉 器

95. Your opponent thinks that you are relaxed, but you are not relaxed: you have inner strength.

歇 鬆 似 非鬆

96. The opponent, sensing your internal strength, thinks that you are tight, but there is no physical strength—it is internal force.

歇 緊 未 着 力

97. All the movement is balanced in a circular fashion.

運 使 求 均 衡

98. The chi is controlled so that it flows in and out in a spiraling circle.

螺 旋 循 環 氣

99. Do not be afraid of the opponent.

達 敵 莫 惶 張

100. Open and close yourself, and be able to yield and stick.

開 闔 收 与 放

101. & 102. Watch for the enemy's weak point, and once discovered, attack without delay.

見 形 尋 破 綻　　絲 毫 不 相 讓

103. The wrist, elbow, shoulder, hip, and knee are all connected.

腕 肘 肩 胯 膝

104. Movements of the legs and hands all work together.

足 蹈 于 腳 齊

105. All the joints work in combination with the geng.

節 節 力 貫 串

106. If this is achieved, there is no chance for the enemy to attack.

處 處 無 飛 陳

107. One's breathing is like the falling of fine cotton.

呼 吸 細 綿 綿

108. Therefore, your breathing can be up or down, slow or fast.

升 降 緩 而 急

109. When this method is mastered, any attack can be met.

得 法 可 應 變

110. Strive for the knowledge of the method, but also the wisdom of its usage.

有 術 方 為 奇

111. Method and wisdom are joined into one.

法 術 二 而 一

112. Both concepts are very important; there cannot be one without the other.

缺 一 不 能 二

113. Both hands rise up lightly.

兩 手 輕 輕 起

114. Bend and stretch fluidly.

曲 伸 無 斷 續

115. All turning and bending is curved.

轉 移 有 曲 折

116. This form is like a swimming dragon at play.

形 似 游 龍 戲

117. Therefore, all sides move up or down, left or right.

縱 橫 与 起 伏

118. This type of exercise follows the way of yin and yang.

陰 陽 運 行 數

119. The idea is formed, and the chi follows.

意 動 氣 相 隨

120. The inner force is concealed within the joints.

關 節 含 蓄 力

121. Relax your muscles, and activate your blood vessels.

舒 筋 活 血 脉

122. This is good for one's health.

榮 衛 得 道 宜

123. When you inhale, your chi rises.

一 吸 氣 便 提

124. When you exhale, the chi sinks to your tan t'ien.

氣 氣 可 歸 臍

125. As soon as the chi rises, it is swallowed and sinks down.

一 提 氣 便 咽

126. In the flow of chi, fire from below and water from above meet harmoniously.

水 火 得 相 見

127. Carefully study this inside and outside kung fu.

精 研 內 外 功

128. The mind (heart) should be empty; the abdomen should be solid.

心 虛 腹 要 實

129. At the moment of opportunity, attack at once.

卒 然 取 其 勢

130. The beginning and the end of hardness and softness are inseparable.

首 尾 不 相 離

131. The outside force and inside force are mutually interchangeable.

奇 正 得 相 生

132. Activity and inactivity follow one's will.

動 靜 隨 心 欵

133. & 134. For those who set out to learn this exercise, do not misjudge the value of the Five-Word Song.

麤 成 五 字 誤　　後 學 莫 輕 視

Stop the Horse at the Cliff

# ~4~

# The History of Hwa Yu

The techniques and metaphysics that evolved into Hwa Yu and the other forms of t'ai chi first appeared in China well over three thousand years ago. These early forms of internal kung fu resembled the Chi Kung "breath control" exercises developed by Confucian monks in the fourth century BC, and later adopted and expanded upon by the taoists. None of these earliest forms of internal martial arts are known to exist today; documentation on them has always been either extremely poor or completely nonexistent. Chen Hsi-I may have been one of the first masters to link taoist longevity practices with martial arts to create internal kung fu (nei chia). Hsing-I, Pa Kua, and most of the t'ai chi systems known today were developed sometime between the late Sung Dynasty (1200AD) and the early Ming Dynasty, (around 1400AD). Although the name t'ai chi was used quite early on, Chen's style, which was created in the 1200s, was the first complete martial system documented to exist under that name.

Hwa Yu's founder, Chen Hsi-I, was a taoist monk, born in the year 906AD in the village of Ching Yun, located in the Ho Chow district of Shensi province, in Northern China. Chen was born to an aristocratic family, and after failing his exam to become an officer of the court, took solace in the hermit's life by living in recluse high atop Mt. Hwa Yu, also located in Northern China. Even as a teenager, Chen Hsi-I had been a noted prodigy and scholar. Before settling on Mt. Hwa Yu, he spent a considerable period of time traveling throughout China, studying with various teachers and philosophers. The fact that he was a respected scholar and expert in the I Ching from an early age helped to open up many doors for Chen, affording him the opportunity to study many esoteric taoist and buddhist disciplines and practices, as well as various martial arts.

Hwa Yu is one of five sacred mountains in Shensi maintained as shrines to honor a group of individuals—dubbed the Immortal Taoist Monks—and the martial arts they developed on those mountains. Chen Hsi-I was one of these great immortals, and along with Chen San Feng of Wu Tang, he originated many of the internal kung fu practices that we know today.

Chen Hsi-I was born Chen Tuan, and often was referred to as Chen Po, a nickname referring to his place of birth. At some point after giving up his aspirations to become a high government official, Chen traveled to Wu Tang hoping to perfect his skills in martial arts and taoist alchemy. It is believed that he went to a place on Mt. Wu Tang called The Rock of Nine Rooms, where he honed his skills in Chi Kung and other forms of taoist meditation, as well as the martial arts. At this time he also learned the taoist art of "Hibernation," which later enabled him to create a set of dream exercises that earned him the title of the "Sleeping Immortal."

Chen developed a reputation for being a great scholar and warrior, and because of this reputation members of the royal court often sought him out. The emperor, Shih Tsung became threatened by this practice and had Chen imprisoned, believing that he fostered desires to take over the empire. After Chen had been imprisoned for one hundred days, Emperor Tsung summoned the sentry who was assigned to guard Chen's cell. Upon hearing from the guard that Chen spent all of his time sleeping—and had not woken up even once—the emperor concluded that Chen wasn't really a threat to his authority, he ordered Chen's release. Chen had forsaken any such lofty desires of men years earlier, after failing his exam to become a high court official. His only wish now was to return to his scenic retreat on Mt. Hwa Yu and be left alone to study and live in peace.

It was at this time that Chen Hsi-I is believed to have invented the arts of Hwa Yu/Liu He Ba Fa and the T'ai Chi Ruler. Some scholars that believe Chen Hsi-I was the teacher of Chen San Feng, the fabled founder of t'ai chi. Because of the time span between them, however, it makes more sense that one of Chen Hsi-I's disciples, Huo Lung, was actually Chen San Feng's teacher. It was much later, around the year 960 that the first Sung emperor, Sung T'ai Tzu, gave Chen Tuan the title Chen Hsi-I, which means "Rare Among Men." It is also believed that after spending considerable time as a recluse, perfecting his skills, Chen Hsi-I returned to Wu Tang and served as an instructor for a period of time in order to perpetuate the taoist ideals in which he believed. He also continued to pass on his knowledge of the I Ching, and much of what we know about this important work today can be credited to Chen's teachings.

There is a story in Chinese lore of how the emperor Chen Hong Yuen had long held a deep admiration for the prowess and reputation that Chen Hsi-I possessed as a kung fu warrior. The emperor asked Chen to assist him in developing his strategy for an upcoming series of battles. Although Chen was indeed an expert in kung fu, as well as a unique and scholarly thinker, his personal beliefs compelled him to refuse the emperor's bidding. As a taoist monk, Chen Hsi-I was not interested in helping his emperor inflict widespread carnage and devastation through war. Chen believed that honoring this request would generate a cataclysm of negative karma, for both himself and his emperor. However, because he was a wise man, Chen Hsi-I didn't want to refuse the emperor outright and create any bad blood between them, so he invited Chen Hong Yuen to a chess match. Chen then offered him a wager: if Chen won the match, the emperor would give him the title to the Hwa Shan mountain range; if he lost, he would relent and help the emperor defeat his enemies. Chen Hsi-I was certainly no fool—he easily defeated the emperor, whose mind was preoccupied with thoughts of his enemies and the upcoming battles. With his clever plan Chen Hsi-I obtained a large plot of land free of charge, and, at the same time, passively helped his emperor by showing him his weakness. Atop Mt. Hwa Ya, a shrine still stands today marking the exact location of the match.

There are other such stories about Chen Hsi-I, however, most of them are either myth or legend, and not necessarily true. What is important is the legacy of martial arts and philosophical concepts that he left behind to posterity through his known disciple Li Tung Fung. According to this legend, Li Tung Fung traveled to Hwa Yu in search of Chen's legacy; he found Chen's cave dwelling, which still contained his remains and written works, and Li used these writings to master Hwa Yu. It is more plausible that Li had been a student of Chen's at some point, either on Hwa Yu or while Chen was teaching at Wu Tang. But either way, though the passing of the art from Chen Hsi-I to Li Tung Fung is hazy at best, the lineage from Li forward is fairly well documented. The fact that Hwa Yu was a "closed-door art" and kept secret except for select individuals makes this lineage easy to follow.

Li Tung Fung lived on Mt. Qi Yun in Anhui province. After discovering Chen's manuscripts, and mastering the art of Hwa Yu with the help of some monks who were residing at Mt. Hwa Yu, Li returned to Anhui, where he passed on the art to Sung Yuen Tung.

## *A brief list of masters who followed Sung Yuen Tung*

- Kwan Kit

- Lan Wan Sing

- Wong Tak Wai

- T'ai Yai Chin, a student of Wong Tak Wai and the first instructor who was known to refer to the art as "swimming boxing." (The terms water and spirit were sometimes used synonymously because it was believed that water was a great source of energy and spirit.)

- Yeung King Kun from Fon Shan, who referred to the art as the "Twelve Movements of Exercise Before Birth."

- Following Yeung, the art was passed on to a disciple known only as Master Shut, who called it "Idea Six Combinations."

- Chen Kong Ta from the town of Yellow Flower in the Hopei Province, a student of Master Shut. Chen Kong Ta called the exercise either "Idea Six Combinations" or "Idea Spiritual Kung Fu."

Unfortunately this list of Hwa Yu's masters is not complete; however, it will give us a basic idea of the history of the art and how it was handed down.

## *Contemporary Instructors*

(Please note that there are other very qualified teachers who are not mentioned here because they do not fall within a direct lineage either to me or to my instructor.)

The first instructor known to "open the door" and bring Hwa Yu to the general public was Wu Yik Fan (1887–1961). Wu was from Tieling, in Northeast China, and later lived in Beijing. He grew up in an aristocratic family that followed scholarly pursuits, and which also blessed him with a varied social life and the means to travel. This affluence afforded him the opportunity to learn calligraphy and painting, as well as the martial arts. In 1896 his family moved to Pienliang. It was here that Wu became heavily involved in the martial arts, learning Hwa Yu/Liu He Ba Fa and also Chen Hsi-I's Taoist Sleeping Chi Kung, along with various other martial systems. It was the teachings of Master Chen Kuang Ti that helped Wu Yik Fan greatly improve his martial ability. While attending the Military Academy of Baoding in 1905, Wu further advanced his martial arts skills under Grand Master Chen Hulou.

Master Wu first began teaching martial arts at South Senior High School in Shanghai in 1928. In 1932, the YMCA in the Eight Immortal Bridge District hired him as their martial arts director. A year later Master Wu moved to the National Martial Arts Association in Nanking, where he served until the Japanese invasion of China. He left Nanking and eventually ended up in Hanoi, Vietnam after being invited there by the Vietnamese government to demonstrate Chinese martial arts. After the war, Wu returned to Shanghai were he resumed teaching, and for the first time provided instruction to students from foreign countries such as Brazil, England, and the United States. It has been documented that Master Wu was a humble and pleasant man who didn't like to show off his talents. Wong Heng Chai, the founder of I Ch'uan (a specific school of Hsing I), classified Wu as one of only three great martial artists he had ever met.

Wu Yik Fan's successor was Shanghai industrialist Chen Yik Yan. Chen was introduced to Master Wu through his friend General Chang Chih-Chiang. At first Chen held the misconception that Hwa Yu/ Liu He Ba Fa was similar to the other T'ai Chi styles taught throughout the city; however, after closer scrutiny, he discovered the full complexity and uniqueness of the art. Chen's social status provided him with the means to follow Master Wu to Nanking to continue his studies during Wu's tenure at the Ching Wu Institute. During his years in Nanking, Chen met and studied with other internal stylists as well. After the Communist takeover of mainland China, Chen moved his practice to Hong Kong, where he began teaching martial arts. He eventually wound up in Singapore, where he remained until his retirement in the late 1950s. It was only after some ardent persuasion by a group of persistent young martial arts students that Master Chen decided to come out of retirement and begin teaching again. Chen continued teaching throughout the 1960s and 1970s; his successor was Wai Lan Choi, who now resides in the United States.

Li John Chung (John Li) was a student of Chen Yik Yan's, while Chen was teaching in Hong Kong in the 1950s and 1960s. Li also studied with two other prominent internal masters, training first with Fang Pak Xing, who concentrated his practice on the t'ai chi aspect of Hwa Yu, and later with Master Han Xing Yaun, who was a Hsing I master specializing in I Ch'uan school of Hsing I. Li's hybrid version of Hwa Yu/ Liu He Ba Fa is believed to hold truer to Chen Hsi-I's original principles—defined in the Six Combinations and Eight Methods—than the styles commonly being taught by other instructors. He called this hybrid version Hwa Yu, in honor of its place of origin.

After living in Hong Kong for more than sixty years, John Li relocated to Boston in the early 1970s, where he opened a school called the Hwa Yu Health Institute. He operated the school for about six years before retiring to Florida in 1978. He returned to Boston a few years later, where he passed away in 1982.

John Li began his martial arts studies as a boy; the first style he learned was Tom Tui (a Northern style of external kung fu), and he continued to practice this and other styles until his death. In his youth, he earned a reputation for being a fierce fighter and skilled exponent of external kung fu; later on, he began studying the internal arts. Li was knowledgeable in the Wu and Yang styles of t'ai chi, as well as Hwa Yu. Li excelled at his scholarly pursuits, and this helped him to become a superior student and teacher of the martial arts. Li taught his t'ai chi program at some of New England's most elite universities, such as Yale, Harvard, MIT, and Boston College.

Although Li had many good students, he decided to pass his lineage along to Robert Xavier. Master Xavier currently resides in Florida, where he actively teaches the art of Hwa Yu T'ai Chi. As of 2005, Master Xavier had almost fifty years of martial arts experience; he is knowledgeable in jiujitsu, judo, karate, and jukido as well as Hwa Yu. He also holds a tenth-degree black belt and is the present lineage holder in Yon Ch'uan martial arts. Master Xavier has taught his art to thousands of children through schools, summer camps, church associations, and mentoring programs. He also developed and documented a system called "Three-Zone Self-Defense," which he taught to police officers throughout Connecticut in the 1970s.

## *Chen Hsi-I's T'ai Chi Ruler*

The T'ai Chi Ruler/Chi Kung exercises that Chen Hsi-I created are also still practiced today. Chen taught the exercise to King Chao in order to help preserve Chao's health, and the exercises passed down through the Chao family lineage.. The T'ai Chi Ruler is a system of Chi Kung or internal kung fu exercises that are performed while holding a specially designed batonlike mechanism, approximately one foot in length, called the T'ai Chi Ruler. The purpose of the Ruler is to help activate the chi flow within the body by absorbing and storing chi so that it can act as a catalyst during future workouts. The physical exercises are similar in nature to Hwa Yu's Rowing exercise, with a few subtle differences.

Glenn and Karen in Standing position.

# ~5~

# Warm-Ups and Rooting Exercises

Although it's not mandatory, it is extremely beneficial, and therefore recommended, that students of Hwa Yu perform a brief warm-up routine consisting of stretching and limbering exercises prior to practice session. The purpose of these exercises is to get the heart pumping faster in order to speed up circulation, and to stretch and loosen up both the cartilage and ligaments (sinews) that support the major joints and the major muscles of the body. Warming-up properly can help prevent possible injuries brought on by sudden exertion. A further advantage derived from stretching is that when the body is limber and circulation increases, one's chi will be prone to rise more expeditiously and more profoundly during practice. Following a daily stretching routine will condition a student's body quicker, which in turn will enable him or her to learn the fundamental exercises and skills of Hwa Yu at a faster pace. Stretching also relaxes the body and helps eliminate or remove pent-up tension and stress. On a personal note, I find that doing a moderate stretching routine just before bedtime helps me to get a better night's sleep.

The warm-up routine that I prefer consists of some quick and simple exercises for limbering the major joints of the body, followed by a series of stretches designed to loosen first the legs, then the upper and lower sections of the torso. This routine also contains exercises that stretch the back of the legs (the hamstrings and calves) and the hip joints, followed by stretches designed to work both the upper and lower regions of the spine. Side bends and twisting exercises are included to help stretch and strengthen the abdominal oblique muscles, which are extremely important for structural support. The final group of exercises is for the shoulders, or rotator cuffs, which are common problem areas for many professional athletes and older individuals.

Although t'ai chi itself is a stretching exercise, one would surely profit from the added benefits of a warm-up routine such as the one I have described here, because the very essence of t'ai chi requires that you to remain as relaxed and limber as possible. I would like to reemphasize that it is the combination of the two, stretching and regular t'ai chi practice, that will yield the maximum results. None of my fellow martial art students succeeded in reaching the level of flexibility that I was able to achieve by combining frequent practice in Hwa Yu with daily stretching routines.

L1

L2

# Limbering Exercises

We begin our warm-up routine with joint-loosening exercises. The purpose of these exercises is to insure that the major joints are in proper working order and to prepare them for the impact of our workout. We start with the ankles and work our way up the body to the neck.

The first joint exercise is shown in photo L1. Support your body weight on either leg and lift the other leg up in front of you along your midline by raising your knee until your thigh is parallel to the floor. Turn the supporting foot out away from your midline, so that it's at a forty-five degree angle, and bend the supporting knee so that your center of gravity lowers. Place your hands on your hips. Allow the raised foot to hang down naturally, and then turn the foot in circles first to the right and then to the left. Change legs and repeat this with the other foot. The size of the circle depends on your degree of flexibility; don't strain the sinews by overextending. (If you feel any sharp pain or if you experience pain after your workout is finished, you have overstretched.)

The second joint exercise, shown in photo L2, is for limbering the knees. Place your heels together and point your toes outward, away from your midline, by forty-five degrees. Place your hands on your knees as shown, and make small lateral circles with the knees, first in one direction and then in the other. It is important that you keep your circles small so that you don't put excessive stress on the crucial ligaments that support the outside of the knee joints.

The third exercise in this set (L3) is for the hips. Place your feet shoulder-width apart and point the toes straight ahead. Place your hands on your hips and make large circles with your hips, first to the right and then to he left.

We now move up to the trunk or torso. This next exercise (L4) works the abdominal oblique muscles and the spine. Form your hands into fists and turn your forearms upward so that your knuckles point toward the ceiling. Then rotate your shoulders and torso as far as you can, first to the right, and then to the left. Move freely and loosely; move quickly but not with force. It is important that you turn your head to the side along with your shoulders as you rotate your torso, and look over your shoulder in the direction that you are turning.

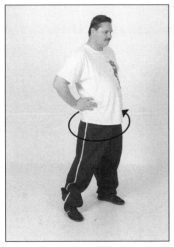  

L3            L4            L5

The last exercise in the first set demonstrates the correct way to loosen up the neck. Stand with your feet shoulder-width apart and place your hands on your hips. Then tilt your head sideways (L5), first toward your right shoulder, and then toward your left shoulder. Repeat this three times. Next, tilt your head forward, pulling your chin down toward your chest, and then lift your chin up once again and tilt your head back. Repeat this three times as well. Remember that these are just limbering exercises, so it is not necessary to overstrain yourself when performing any of these routines, especially when working the knees and the neck area.

## Stretching Exercises

For the second set in this warm-up routine we'll once again start with our legs and move up to the torso.

To stretch the hip flexors and groin muscles, start by standing with your feet shoulder-width apart. Squat all the way down to the floor, and place both hands on the floor in front of you for support. Extend either leg to one side, keeping the foot pointing straight ahead (L6). Then pull your toes back and up toward your body and push your heel out. Now, moderately push down into the hip of the extended leg. Release the pressure by rising up a little, then sink down again. After completing four or five repetitions, switch sides and do the same thing on the other leg. When you switch legs, don't stand up: simply push your torso across so that it is positioned over the other foot. This gives your hips a little extra work.

L6  L7

The next exercise is designed to work the back of the legs: the hamstrings and the calf muscles. Squat into position as you did in the previous exercise; however, when you extend your leg rotate the foot straight up toward the ceiling and turn your torso so that you are facing the upturned foot. Keeping your back straight, lower your torso forward toward the extended leg as far as you can (L7). Go slowly, and don't jerk into the stretch. Repeat this five times and then curl your back a little and bring just your head down. This works the spine. Switch legs and repeat this on the other side.

We complete our leg stretches by sitting on the floor and spreading our feet as far apart as possible, known as the spread eagle position (L8). Turn your torso toward your left foot and lower yourself as close to it as possible (L9), then turn to the other leg and repeat the same thing. Again, move at a moderate or slow pace. You can do as many repetitions of this as you wish. Lastly, finish by turning your torso back to the center so that you are facing straight ahead. Keeping your back as straight as you can, lower your torso and try to reach the ground with your chest (L10). Don't be too discouraged if you have a hard time doing this or find that you can only get halfway down, as this exercise takes considerable practice.

I like to follow this exercise by practicing some splits, however, this is totally optional. First I perform a straddle or side split, and then I turn forty-five degrees and do a front split. Photo L11 shows a front split. To do side splits safely, start out supporting yourself with your hands and move very slowly. At first, don't try to go for the maximum stretch—stop at eighty percent. For the front split, start with your back knee on the floor, and then slowly try to extend the stretch further.

L8

L9

L10

L11

L12

L13

L14

The first exercise in the upper-body series is called the cat stretch. It stretches the upper back (thoracic area) and the shoulders. Begin by stretching your arms straight out in front of you, at chest height, and tucking your head down in between your outstretched arms (L12). Hunch your upper spine back like a cat as you drop your head down between your elbows. Next, raise both arms straight up toward the ceiling and make your spine as long and straight as you can (L13). Keeping your arms raised, finish the exercise by forming your hands into fists and pushing your elbows back as you stick out your chest (L14). You should do this stretch very slowly.

L15

The second exercise in this set works the lumbar area (lower back) and the shoulders. Stand with your feet approximately 1½ times shoulder-width apart (to measure this, multiply the distance from one shoulder to the next by 1½ times). Raise your hands straight up (L15), then bend forward and sweep your hands between your feet (L16). Next, raise your torso back up to a standing position while sweeping your hands above your head and pointing your arms straight to the ceiling (L17). Lastly, turn the palms of your hands toward the ceiling with the fingers spread out and arch your back (L18). You should stretch back to about ninety percent of your maximum capability. Returning to an upright position (L15) completes the first repetition of this exercise. I usually do ten repetitions at a medium speed.

L16                        L17                        L18

The last upper-body exercise is a side bend. Stand with your feet slightly wider than shoulder-width apart, and stretch your arms straight out to each side, palms facing the floor. Lean to your right, letting your right palm slide down along your right leg; at the same time, bring your left hand over your head and push the palm as far to the right as possible. Return to a standing position and repeat the same movement on your left side. Again, I recommend ten repetitions (stretching both sides equals one repetition).

This is just a quick and simple routine to prepare you for t'ai chi practice. Other exercises can certainly be added to this routine: For example, I usually add a set of alternating toe touches and some other abdominal or back exercises.

# Rooting

The rooting exercises are the first set of skills taught to a new student of Hwa Yu. The rooting exercises develop a strong foundation, or base of support, that will improve an individual's balance and power by developing core movement and creating whole-body unity. These factors will enable a student to perform all of the ensuing movements of Hwa Yu with greater accuracy and proficiency.

Rooting exercises strengthen and increase the flexibility of ligaments and cartilage within the lower joints (knees, ankles, and hips), as well as strengthen the leg muscles. Finally, rooting will help beginners learn the basic "rounds" (structural alignment) of the body: the back is rounded, the arms are round as if hugging, the legs are bowed as if they were two mighty oak trees bending in the wind, the chest is hollowed, and the hands are rounded as if they are the tiger's mouth. An important reminder: always maintain a relaxed posture while practicing Hwa Yu.

## *Rowing*

The first exercise in this group is called Rowing (as in rowing a boat).

R1 Rowing, Neutral Stance     R2 Rowing, Weight Shift

## STEPPING INTO ROWING POSITION

1. Start in a neutral position (R1). This is a "double-weighted" stance, which means that each leg supports fifty percent of your body weight. This stance is only used at the beginning and end of an exercise or form.

2. To step from a neutral position into a rowing stance you must first turn either one of your feet (left or right) away from your midline by forty-five degrees (R2). Note that in figures R2 through R7, I have turned my right foot outward and shifted my body weight onto my right leg (R2).

R3 Rowing, Centering the Foot        R4 Rowing, Advancing the Foot

3. The knee of your supporting leg should bend until it is over the toes of the corresponding foot, and your midline should shift from the center to the inside edge of the right foot. This will leave the left foot, which is now called the "stepping foot," light or "empty." (Remember most of your body weight is now being supported entirely by your right leg.)

When your stepping foot is light, or weightless, it can be moved effortlessly and without affecting your balance. Now, slide the left foot across toward the right foot until the heel is lined up with the toes of the right foot, and positioned in front of the right heel (R3). Your body weight remains balanced over your right foot. From this position, slide your left foot, which is the stepping foot, straight ahead—I like to imagine my foot following an invisible line on the floor. This forward movement stops once your left leg has straightened to approximately ninety percent of its maximum reach

(R4). You should never fully extend the advancing leg because this would place excess stress on your joints, especially on the forward knee. Note that in photo R4 my right knee is bent quite a lot and my left knee is also slightly bent and relaxed. Lastly, slide or step the left foot straight across to the left once again, so that the insteps of both feet end up shoulder-width apart as they started out in figure R1. Now you are ready to learn the Rowing movement.

## THE ROWING MOVEMENT

1. Tuck your tailbone and your buttocks muscles under and forward, as though you were tucking your tail between your legs. Keep your legs bowed outward so that each knee is over the midline of its corresponding foot. With the legs bowed in this manner it is easy to press the outside edges of the feet firmly to the ground (R5); this provides maximum stability and adds peripheral balance to your stance. Next, relax your chest by letting it sink into a concave position. Remember to remain relaxed and keep yourself from tensing up as you collapse your chest inward. This sinking is called "hollowing the chest." The "hollowing," combined with the pelvic tilt created by tucking in the tailbone, will give the back a rounded appearance. It is also important to remember to keep your torso erect, or plumb, throughout the entire exercise. Your hips should remain directly under your shoulders, or on the same vertical plane (i.e., do not lean either forward or backward). When you perform this exercise, it is also necessary to remain square or centered, so that your hips and shoulders face directly to the front at all times.

R5 Rowing, Stepping Wider    R6 Rowing, Back Stance    R7 Rowing, Forward Stance

2. Notice that I placed my hands on my hips as I stepped into my Rowing stance (R1-R5). Now, drop your hands to your sides and relax your arms. To bring them into Rowing position scoop the hands inward and up, as though you were scooping up a pile of leaves. Continue raising the hands upward until they reach the level of your diaphragm (just below your heart), and then let the hands gently open by spreading them outward until they are once again shoulder-width apart. As you open the hands, turn the palms downward so that they end up facing the floor (like spreading the waves). Keep your arms rounded and your elbows bowed out as you move your hands into position. Once your hands are in position, turn your thumbs slightly upward until each hand is at a fifteen-degree pitch (R6 & R7).

   Your shoulders should hang downward naturally and they should remain relaxed. Keep the roundness in your arms (as if you are holding a large beach ball), and then let your elbows hang downward slightly. If you have done everything correctly, your hands should now be slightly higher than your elbows. Stretch up the crown of the head as if you are being pulled from above. This will help your spirit to rise upward, which will increase your energy and smooth out your movements. Internally, stretch outward and upward from your tan t'ien to the tips of your fingers and the crown of your head. Keep your chin tucked back or in slightly and remember that everything you do should feel natural—nothing should ever be forced. You are now ready to "row."

3. Rowing consists of moving back and forth between two stances—front stance and back stance (R6 & R7)—in an elliptical fashion. Start from back stance (R6), gripping the floor lightly with your toes. Using the heel of your right foot for leverage, push your torso downward and forward until your left knee is positioned over your toes; keep your buttocks and tailbone tucked in as you push forward. At this point your left leg should be supporting sixty percent of your total body weight. It is important to keep the torso erect or plumb, as if there was an imaginary line running straight down through your body from the crown of your head, and to move your whole body as one unit. Once your body weight has reached the front leg, push your trunk up and then back again using the heel of your left foot. When your body weight is over the rear leg, tuck in your tailbone and buttocks once again and sit back into your rear hip flexor, as though you were sitting back onto a barstool. It's a good idea to find a kitchen stool, or whatever you have available, and try this a few times to study the movement. At first it may be difficult, and perhaps even painful, to sink deep into the hip flexor, but with continued practice you will

improve, and any pain will soon go away. The biggest mistake that students make is failing to keep the buttocks tucked in, which puts excess strain on the knees. If you keep the buttocks and pelvis tucked under, your hip-flexor muscles will support your body weight, and your knees will not suffer. The rowing motion continues as you move forward again, keeping the pelvis tucked under and your legs bowed.

R8 Rowing, Front Stance

R9 Rowing, Back Stance

4. Your center of gravity rises as you push yourself back, and it sinks as you push yourself forward. The movement is in the shape of an oval (R10). Try to keep your midline moving straight forward and straight backward; don't allow it to waiver from side to side. Keep your shoulders and hips squared and facing front throughout the entire movement.

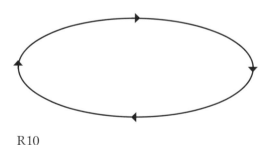

R10

# *Walking*

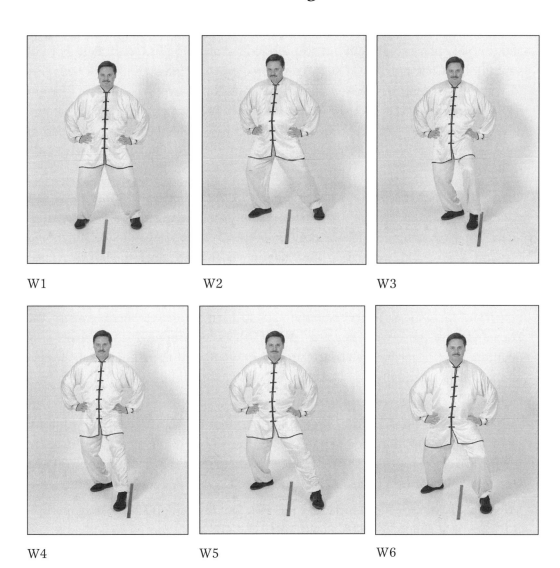

W1   W2   W3

W4   W5   W6

1. The Walking exercise starts with the same neutral stance we used to start our Rowing exercise (W1). Turn your right foot forty-five degrees away from your midline, just as you did at the beginning of Rowing (W2). Slide your left foot across so that its heel lines up alongside the toes of your right foot, and your left heel is just a little ahead of your right heel (W3). Tuck in your buttocks and sit into your right hip flexor. Your left heel lifts up off the floor slightly.

2. Next, sit a little deeper into your hip and slide the left foot straight ahead, just as we did in Rowing (W4). The left foot is now in its forward position, but it's still centered—in line with the inside edge of the right heel. The left knee is about ninety percent straight but still relaxed (or as John Li says, straight but not straight; bent but not bent). Keep your torso erect and centered when stepping forward; never lean or allow your body to tilt. Never overextend your forward leg by stepping so far forward that the knee becomes straight. Everything should always feel like it's very natural. One last item to remember is that the pad of the stepping foot should maintain light contact with the floor as it slides gently forward.

3. Once you have extended your left foot forward, slide it straight across to the left once again (W5), until you are back to standing with your feet shoulder-width apart. Now, tuck the buttocks and tailbone under, as before, and sink down and forward, like we did in Rowing. The body moves forward until the left (forward) knee is over the toes of the left or forward foot (W6). Your hands and arms should scoop in and up as in Rowing; however, this time they will take a wider position (1½ times as wide as before). Remember to turn the palms down toward the floor and raise the fingers upward (W7-W10). When stepping into the Walking position, the fingers lightly stretch up and outward and the elbows are rounded and sink down a little.

4. We have just completed one step. To continue Walking forward, turn your left foot out forty-five degrees and slide your right foot to your midline and up until your heel lines up alongside the toes of the left foot (W11). Keep your arms in their Walking position until you complete your exercise. It is acceptable to lift and step the right foot into place, but you must keep it very close to the ground.

5. To complete your second step, slide your right foot forward, then wider again until it is back to a shoulder-width position (W12). Once the foot is in position, row down and forward until the right knee is over the toes of the right foot (W13).

6. You can continue Walking forward for as long or as far as you wish, provided you have the space. I like to walk all the way across my backyard, and then walk backward until I have returned to my starting point.

7. To walk backward you have to reverse the whole process. Starting from where we left off in right front, or forward, stance, raise your torso up and back by pushing off the front foot. It's done just like Rowing: you rise up as you go back, and sink

down as you go forward. Next, sit back into your rear hip flexor, and remember to tuck the buttocks in and under.

8. Remain sitting back into your left hip, and slide your right foot straight across until it is in line with the inside edge of your left heel. Then slide or step your right foot straight back until it is positioned slightly ahead of your left foot, as in photo W10. To complete the backward step, slide your right foot back and over to the right, as in photo W9. Remember that when we stepped forward, the foot went straight ahead first and then stepped or moved wider. When you are stepping backward, you follow the same pattern—move the foot first to your center, then back, then behind you and over.

W7

W8

W9

W10

W11

W12

W13

## *Practicing Rowing and Walking*

The point of Walking in this fashion is to maintain your balance, centering, and control throughout the entire exercise. John Li called this exercise "walking like a chicken." The way that most people walk is to swing one leg forward and let their body weight fall on this forward swinging foot. By walking this way they are throwing their center of gravity forward and then recovering their balance as their body catches up to it. In contrast, Hwa Yu Walking teaches you to move the stepping foot inward first so that it stays under your center of gravity, allowing you to always maintain your equilibrium. The method described in this section is the beginning or easiest method of Hwa Yu Walking. It is necessary to practice this method for a significant period of time to improve your balance and strengthen your legs before moving on to a harder or more advanced method. In the second method of Walking you omit one of the transition steps used in the first method, which makes staying balanced throughout the entire exercise a little more difficult. You slide the advancing foot up to meet the heel as in position W3, then slide or step the foot forward and wider in one movement. Walking back could be done using this two-movement method, or if you wish, you could revert back to the first method. In the third and most advanced method of Walking, the whole step is done in one movement. It's important not to move ahead to this method too soon in your training because it requires you to sit very deep into the hips, a maneuver that requires significant practice before it can be achieved.

You need to build up your endurance for both the Rowing and Walking exercises gradually. When a new student starts to learn Rowing, I recommend that they begin with thirty-six cycles, or revolutions, on each side (with the right leg back and then the left). This should take you six to seven minutes per side to complete. You should practice once or twice daily and follow the thirty-six—cycle routine for two to three weeks. Remember that Rowing and Walking are practiced slowly. The Five-Word Song states, "To move seems not to move." (FWS, line 77) Although it is very beneficial to practice at such a slow pace, it is also acceptable to go a little bit faster at first until you get the hang of the movements.

After the third week of training, I have students increase the number of revolutions and the duration of practice gradually until they can row nonstop for thirty minutes on each side. Once a student reaches this plateau, everything changes. At this point, he will start to feel rooted to the ground. He will also start to feel his chi begin to rise up his spine and radiate out along his arms. His body will take on a feeling of lightness and connectedness; he will feel in touch with his surroundings and more intensely notice the things around him.

Walking practice is developed very much the same way; you start out practicing for five to ten- minutes at a time, and build up to 30 minutes nonstop. Once you have reached thirty minutes you can then practice nonstop for an hour, which is the ultimate goal. It isn't necessary to practice longer than one hour, but remember that the more you practice, the better your technique will be. A good schedule is one hour of Rowing in the morning before going off to work, and one hour of Walking before retiring at night. This regimen, combined with a half-hour of regular walking or jogging three times per week, is a near-perfect exercise routine.

## *More on Walking and Rowing*

There is an endless amount of details that could be discussed in regards to Rowing and Walking; I would like to point out some of the more important ones. Your shoulders and hips should remain square and facing front at all times in both Rowing and Walking. When you practice Walking, your centerline moves slightly from side to side as you move from one leg to the other, however, during Rowing, the centerline moves straight forward and straight back only. Notice that in the Walking photographs, we placed a black line on the floor so you can see how my centerline changes from side to side. The shoulders and hips should also remain level at all times; you must be careful not to lean or drop one of your shoulders lower than the other. The torso must remain plumb (vertical) at all times in both exercises. Your tongue should be curled back and placed against the roof of your mouth.

Although the bowing in the legs eases a little as you rise up and row back in both exercises, you must keep the back knee turned out so that it's in line with the toes of the rear foot. In other words, the back knee always points outward by forty-five degrees. The bowing is increased once again as you begin to sit back into your rear hip.

The line from your elbow to your fingertips should be a smooth arc. Be careful not to lift the hands and form a bend at the wrists. Think of it this way: If someone were to push against your fingertips, the joints must be lined up so that the force is pushed straight through your entire body and right down into your tan t'ien. If this alignment is correct, you will be able to turn your spine and send the pusher's force right back into him.

Keep your chin pulled back. And remember that although you should stretch up with the crown of your head, you should not pull your body weight up with your head. You must keep the weight down in your lower abdomen in order to stay rooted.

When you bow your legs and knees you should feel the outside edges of your feet press into the floor. The yin-yang theory is employed in all areas of the body when practicing Hwa Yu; in accordance with this, your weight distribution should be sixty percent on the heels and forty percent on the balls of the feet. This is yet another reason why it's important to lightly grip the floor with your toes, and push from your heels when propelling your torso forward or backward. The ultimate goal is whole-body unity. Once you achieve this coordination, you will have gained the ability to either push or pull an adversary with great force. When you are Rowing backward you can visualize that you are pulling or drawing your attacker's energy forward, and when you are Rowing forward you can visualize that you are pushing him or her away from you.

## *Standing*

S1 Standing, Low Position  S2 Standing, Middle Position  S3 Standing, High Position

Standing (Nia Kung) is the last of the three rooting exercises. It is the most important of the three for the development of geng, the internal force. This geng is sometimes referred to as a "trigger force" because once expressed it springs forth instantly. Your spirit, or will, directs the geng, which works in conjunction with the chi. This internal force is both wonderful and powerful. When you practice Rowing and Walking, you increase the flow of chi within your body. The chi is stored in the tan t'ien when it is not being used; during practice, the chi rises up and circulates throughout the body. Your body will then manifest geng by compressing the chi stored within the tan t'ien downward and then forcing this chi back up into the spine and subsequently to all of the body's bones and sinews. The Standing exercise is the vehicle that will manifest geng in the shortest amount of time. Therefore, it is important to practice Standing early on in order to obtain the greatest benefit from Hwa Yu, whether for its therapeutic value or its self-defense capabilities.

Standing, as its name infers, is stillness, meaning you assume a single position and remain in this position for the duration of the exercise. There are seven common Standing postures; however, almost any position in the Hwa Yu form could be used as a standing exercise. The above illustrations (S1–S3), demonstrate three of the most commonly used Standing postures. To get into these postures, start from the neutral position as we did in both the Rowing and Walking exercises. You can also move your feet wider, approximately 1½ times your own shoulder width, which will enable you to sit deeper into your hips, forcing your hip flexors to work harder. You sit into this Standing posture by tucking in the buttocks and the tailbone, bowing your legs so that the outside edges of your feet are pushed into the floor, and sitting back into your hips. Remember: it's like sitting back onto a stool. Grip your toes lightly into the floor without hyperextending your arches (i.e, curling your feet to much). Next, hollow your chest as in Rowing, and let your weight fall to the tan t'ien. It's important to keep all parts of your body that are above the tan t'ien light (as if they are floating on air), and stretch up your head from the crown. This will raise your spirit, which in turn will help to raise your internal force.

Photo S1 shows the arms and hands in the lowest position. This position enables you to focus on the legs because the arms are relaxed and won't require a lot of effort to maintain their position. As you sit back into your stance, let the arms swing forward from your hips about nine inches. Your palms should be turned inward toward one another forming a large circle; once you've got this in place, just drop your elbows back slightly while keeping the roundness in the arms. Your entire arm should form one smooth continuous curve or arch; it is important not to let either your elbow or wrist bend and form a kink. This curvature of the arms works in the same manner as a garden hose, if you put a kink in the hose the water flow diminishes or stops completely. This same thing would happen to your chi if you bent your elbow, losing the evenness of your arm's arc. While standing in this position, let the chi rise up toward the crown of your head and circulate through the loop formed by your arms. As you inhale, bring the chi up your back through your spine; as you exhale, let the chi sink back down the front of your body along your midline to the tan t'ien. "One's breathing is like the falling of fine cotton." (FWS, line 107) Your legs, as well as any body part located below the tan t'ien, will become heavy like the earth. At first your legs will ache and feel the strain of supporting your entire body weight, but if you persevere and work through this pain, eventually any soreness or discomfort will fade away. Holding this position may even begin to energize you and give you a feeling of extreme elation, almost as if you were high—naturally high, that is.

This is the very essence of Standing, which is also referred to as stance training. The martial arts by nature require sophisticated upright movement, which requires a high degree of natural balance. Hwa Yu takes these demands to their extreme. Under normal circumstances the body's sensory mechanisms and psychomotor mechanisms adjust as necessary to balance and support our body weight. All of this is done without requiring any conscious thought from us. During Standing the muscles, tendons, and ligaments that are used unconsciously by the body for balance and structural support are worked to exhaustion. Once these muscles, which are normally used for structural support, are exhausted, the body will activate the (previously untapped) deeper muscle tissue for help with this task. Daily practice gradually develops and increases the body's load-bearing capability. The erector muscles that support the spine are also developed in this same manner.

S4                                           S5                                           S6

As we did with Rowing and Walking, we begin by Standing for thirty-six cycles—in this case, the amount of time it takes to draw thirty-six breaths—then gradually increase the duration of our practice. The ultimate goal is to be able to stand for one full hour each day. It's best to start out easy, and gradually increase your Standing practice by five minutes per week. Remember: just as in your Walking and Rowing practice, once you are able to stand for a full thirty minutes, it will be easy to increase your time up to one hour. It is also important to remember to keep the fingers lightly touching together and open your thumb from the index finger in-order to form the Tiger's Mouth (S3 depicts the Tiger's Mouth the best). If you're feeling exceptionally tired, don't push yourself—this is your body's way of telling you it isn't ready to hold the posture for so long. Remember, everything should feel natural.

Photos S2 and S4 show the hands and arms being held in a mid-level position. Bringing your hands up to a higher position—which is much more difficult—will create two new terminals into which the chi can rise. As you raise your arms and hands higher, the majority of your chi will rise higher as well (S3 & S6). When Standing in the first position (S1) the chi will begin to rise to the arms and the crown of the head; raising the arms up higher acts as a catalyst to draw the chi up faster. In the second Standing position (S2) your fingers should be about even with your diaphragm, and your elbows should hang downward, about even with your lower ribcage. The third Standing position (S3) shows the arms at their highest level. In this position your fingertips are at the level of your eyebrows. John Li would constantly remind us to keep our elbows low, and our arms and back rounded. Photograph S6 shows the roundness of the back from a side view.

When you first start to practice Standing, you will naturally focus on your form, but as you improve and get more comfortable with your Standing postures, you must learn to empty your mind of all thoughts and let your spirit rise up. As you progress to this level, you can learn to concentrate on your breathing, which will help raise and smooth out your chi. Breathe in lightly from the tan t'ien, or bottom of the abdomen, and imagine your breath moving upward to the heart; when you exhale, imagine pushing your breath from the heart downward to the tan t'ien. The Five-Word Song states, "All breathing should be natural from the bottom of the abdomen to the heart. One's breathing is like the falling of fine cotton." (FWS, lines 37, 44 & 107) As you inhale, feel the chi rise up with your breath, spreading out to the tips of your fingers and the crown of your head. As you exhale, push down into your hips and let the chi sink into the tan t'ien. Remember to bow the legs as you sink down into your hips. When you sit lower your center of gravity drops, which makes your stance more rooted. One last detail to remember is to keep your feet pointing straight ahead; do not allow the toes to turn out even the slightest amount.

Master Xavier and myself in a stance from Green Dragon Stretches his Claws.

# ~6~

# The Hwa Yu Long Form:
# General Instructions & Sections One
# and Two of the Form

"Once the enemy is offensive, he is defeated." (FWS, line 67) This line from the Five-Word Song characterizes the no-nonsense approach to self-defense that Hwa Yu personifies. If you remain balanced, calm, and centered both mentally and physically, you will find that any attack initiated by your opponent will create an opening upon which you can capitalize. Each technique is designed to instantaneously lead your adversary to the position in which you have the greatest amount of control over him or her. The principal method that a Hwa Yu player employs in order to gain control of an attacker is called "quartering." In quartering, you maneuver your opponent into a position that greatly reduces his attack options and leaves him with only one of his major weapons accessible (i.e., one arm or one foot or leg). Quartering is achieved either by redirecting your attacker with your block or by repositioning yourself away from the attacker's advance. If you remain centered as you "quarter" your opponent, all of your weapons will remain available and in position for you to counterattack your assailant. In short, Hwa Yu teaches you to neutralize your opponent's weapons thus giving you a tremendous advantage over him or her. Once you've practiced your rooting exercises, and achieved the correct balance and centering, you're ready to learn the forms and their corresponding self-defense applications.

The principles contained within the Six Combinations and Eight Methods are paramount for building ultimate self-defense capability. To put these philosophies to work, you must actively employ the principles while practicing the forms. Remember that the ultimate goal is to thoroughly relax your body and to create a strong unity between your mind, body, and spirit. Line 4 of the Five-Word Song states, "With a calm mind, one is free from hesitation." The freedom of movement brought on by a calm mind will enable a Hwa Yu student to respond to any attacks with lightning speed and remarkable accuracy. Tension and fear create blocks that hinder and slow down response time. John Li would often use the phrase "slow makes fast." Although this seems like a contradiction, it is not. By training slowly and learning to relax a student develops every cell and muscle fiber in his or her body. This generates lightning fast powerful responses that happen before an attacker knows what hit him. From the Five-Word Song we learn, "One strikes with internal force before the opponent advances with strength." (FWS, line 26) If an opponent attacks solely with physical strength, it will create tension in his body and slow down his attack, which would give the edge to the defender, especially if he or she remains calm and relaxed. Although the opponent's attack may seem fast and furious to the untrained eye, to the Hwa Yu practitioner it will seem as if it's happening in slow motion.

The "whole-body unity" that was discussed earlier, will render such power to your techniques that it will be difficult for an opponent to counter or avoid your responses. All strikes are derived through your roots (your stance) and propelled upward through your spine. You turn your waist by rotating from your kidneys, thereby creating a centrifugal effect and accelerating all of your body's momentum and force forward, into your opponent. You add to this impact by rotating the muscles in your arm as you strike, which will cause them to coil or spiral inward upon impact. This is much like taking a bunch of small fibers and twisting them together—turning them into a rope greatly increases their tensile strength. This natural contraction has an effect like a coiled spring and adds strength and power to your follow-up technique as you release it. This striking power is magnified once again by the addition of your internal force, or geng, to the equation. These factors of proper body structure and core movement make it possible for people of smaller size, such as women, to have the ability to defend themselves against much larger attackers.

As we learned in our rooting section, the hips play a major role in supporting and structuring the body and, ultimately, in any and all movement that stems from this support. The hips, just as the arms, coil and uncoil throughout all of the form's movements. Both add strength to your strikes or blocks as they coil or wind in, and explode like a jack-in-the-box as the coil is released. Whole-body movement is created when you keep the pelvis and spine connected, with the spine held plumb, or vertical. The legs stay bowed throughout the exercise to enable weight transitions to be smooth and effortless. This smooth movement will greatly inhibit your opponent's ability to keep track of where you are as he tries to attack you. He'll think you are in one place, but upon advancing, he'll suddenly find you in a different spot. Most karate schools, and many other systems or schools of martial arts, teach their practitioners to straighten or lockout their back leg in order to brace themselves and form a strong stance. Although this practice has some degree of effectiveness, keeping the legs bowed or rounded will provide far better results. The reason for this is that with the legs straight you are bracing yourself on top of the ground (or floor), and by keeping the legs rounded or bowed you will have the ability to sink your roots deep into the ground.

Support is maintained throughout the body by utilizing the concept of "straight but not straight and bent but not bent." This means that even though the legs are bowed, the joints are properly aligned so that the force travels from one to the next without interruption, thereby forming a strong yet flexible structural system that is very similar in concept to the root structure of a tree. If a tree is either too rigid or not rooted deep enough, it will either topple over or crack and break when a strong wind blows. The bowing in the legs also forms a peripheral base of support which helps a Hwa Yu practitioner intercept and divert any oncoming attacks into the empty space (quarter) with relative ease.

The Eight Methods' principle of "return" also plays an important role in forming whole-body unity. (see Chapter 2.) According to this principle, as our torso is pushed forward or backward, the tailbone tucks in and up and the chest hollows, thereby causing the spine to coil and create a counterbalance by initiating a spiraling effect whereby all parts of the body rotate around the center axis, the t'an tien. Remember that whenever the body is in motion, all body parts come into play. When one body part advances it must be offset or counterbalanced by another body part sinking or rotating backward.

"Whether to attack or to protect is according to one's own decision" (FWS, line 30). "Take the first opportunity and be quicker than the opponent" (FWS, line 31). These two lines tell us to advance quickly if we can, before our adversary has a chance to mount a powerful attack. If your opponent's attack is too swift or too forceful, you must first yield to the oncoming force and divert it, leading the attack into "emptiness." As soon as your opponent's attack has been neutralized, you can follow up immediately with the appropriate counterattack. By yielding, you are not retreating from a hopeless cause but simply creating the necessary space to once again put yourself in a commanding position.

Hwa Yu's techniques are often very subtle, consisting of a simple arm turn, a seemingly insignificant spinal twist, or a small drop in hip placement. However, each of these inconspicuous maneuvers can have a tremendous impact on an attacker. A subtle turn of the forearm—and a minimal amount of exertion—can forcefully repel an incoming punch or kick. It's even possible for a small person to parry and fend off a strong attack, such as a hard roundhouse punch, simply by forming the correct alignment, or roundness, with their arms and then turning their torso by rotating from their kidneys. If this movement is performed correctly, they will have quartered their attacker in the process. In other types of martial arts students are taught to defend against this type of attack by using a forearm block—swinging one or both of your arms to meet an oncoming punch. However, this type of blocking technique could result in serious injury to a person of smaller stature and bone structure, especially if they were to execute it against a very strong attacker.

One of Master Xavier's favorite martial arts stories is germane to this exact scenario; he has also indicated that it was the reason he began to question the training he had been so dedicated to for so long and ultimately took up Hwa Yu in its place. One day, while training with a group of students in his former teacher's dojo, Master Xavier witnessed a fairly petite female student (an experienced black belt) execute an outside forearm block in order to defend herself against an oncoming roundhouse punch. The force of the oncoming blow was so strong that it shattered her forearm. The unfortunate results of this unnecessary accident both shocked and sickened Master Xavier and left him with many doubts. Well, the very next week, happened upon an advertisement for one of John Li's seminars, and he decided to travel to Yale University to learn about Hwa Yu. Master Xavier was impressed by what he saw that day, and although he didn't immediately grasp the total efficacy of Hwa Yu, he began taking classes in this new martial art. After he had been training for a while, Master Xavier began to see the great depth and beauty of Hwa Yu, and decided to fully dedicate himself to mastering his newfound art.

The Rowing exercise plays an important role in enabling a student of Hwa Yu to be able to remain in complete control of a confrontation, even while retreating. One of the great things about Hwa Yu is that it allows for its exponents to deliver a devastating or crippling blow while shifting their body back and away from their attacker. Many martial arts systems only teach students to strike an opponent as they move forward into their opponent, but the skills obtained from Hwa Yu's Rowing exercise enable students to pull or push an adversary with great force. Furthermore,

Walking provides students with the ability to block or strike an opponent while in transition between stances, a skill that is useful for preventing practitioners from getting trapped or caught flat-footed. The Five-Word Song verse that illustrates this theory reads, "When in motion, one is still rooted." (FWS, line 23)

A new student will tend to exaggerate all of his or her movements, but as he or she becomes more advanced, the movements will become smaller and more subtle. For example, new students tend to over-rotate their midlines when evading attacks, and they also tend to sit too far back in their stance when Rowing to back stance. An advanced student moves only as far as he must in order to achieve the required results. This minimal movement reduces any recovery time needed for the defender to reestablish his or her center, allowing the defender to execute an immediate counterattack. In most other forms of t'ai chi, exponents will completely empty themselves when yielding by shifting all their body weight back onto one leg. In contrast, students of Hwa Yu are taught to shift only sixty percent of their body weight to their rear leg and to yield through their core. This method leaves them more stable and better prepared to counterattack. "All the joints work in combination with the geng. If this is achieved, there is no chance for the enemy to attack." (FWS, lines 105 & 106)

## The Three C's Principle

The "Three C's" of Hwa Yu are contact, control, and counter. When an opponent attacks with a punch or a kick, the Hwa Yu practitioner blocks the attack by clearing his or her midline (raising either one or both hands up your centerline and turning the elbows outward in order to round the arms). By implementing the block the Hwa Yu practitioner makes contact with the assailant's attacking limb. Remember, maintaining control of your center is vital because it allows you to quarter an opponent and enables you to protect your vital organs. Keeping control of your center is also essential for proper rooting. Although the method of contact (blocking technique) will vary according to the attack, you must always coil your body from your core as you intercept the attack. This coiling action prepares you for the next movement, which is to gain control of your attacker. You achieve control either by drawing the attacker forward, thereby causing him to overextend himself, which puts him off-balance, or by turning and redirecting the attacker's midline (i.e., turning your opponent's centerline away from you, often accomplished by pushing his or her attacking arm off to one side), which places you in a strategic position. The third "C," counter, is the follow-up or immobilization of the attacker. Once control has been established you can retaliate with a striking technique or utilize a joint-locking skill to contain the aggressor. A more advanced practitioner can join contact and control into one motion, and in the highest level of the art, all three components combine into one smooth, efficient motion. This advanced application of the "Three C's" comes from long, hard practice, and by mastering smooth, effortless movement by practicing the forms. Remember that a calm, relaxed state of mind is essential to eliminating any hesitation from your movements.

Training the hip-flexor muscles with the rooting exercises is essential for developing the ability to remain balanced and vertical while performing Hwa Yu. The hip flexors also play a major role in providing power for executing the "Three C's," and they provide the force that enables you to use whole-body motion when you are pushing or pulling an opponent. Controlling your opponent often means controlling his centerline, because if you control his center, you control him. Accordingly, if your opponent is highly skilled and thereby able to maintain command of her center of gravity, you will fail to retain control of her and may end up losing the fight. The more skilled a fighter is, the more difficult it is to lead him off of his center of gravity and gain control.

# Round and Smooth:
# The Essence of the Hwa Yu Movements

All things in nature, such as the seasons and the earth itself, are reliant on cycles or have "roundness." This circularity provides a great source of power and continuity to all things. The roundness of Hwa Yu is what gives it its smoothness, and it is an important source of its power. From the Five-Word Song we learn, "Movement is like an arrow: quick and straight." (FWS, line 34) However, we must remember that the path of the arrow is arced. All our movements should also follow an arced or curved path. A Hwa Yu practitioner learns to move smoothly and evenly: Abrupt or sharp movements are referred to as "telegraphing," and immediately alert the opponent to our intentions, whereas smooth movements give him no warning that he is in any danger. Smooth movements also enable a person to flow from one position or skill to the next without interruption or delay. This creates a continuity of motion, like the tide that ebbs and flows without interruption and which cannot be stopped, all the while conserving the energy of the Hwa Yu practitioner. The Five-Word Song reads, "Conceal one's force like the bow: round and ready to spring." (FWS, line 33)

When striking, the Five-Word Song dictates, "The hands should be seventy percent to the rear and thirty percent to the front." One hand moves forward as the other hand withdraws. The withdrawing or "return hand" initiates the strike by pulling all of your energy down through one side of your body and into your root; the energy then springs up through the other side of your body and out through the "advancing hand." It requires more force for the "return hand" to initiate a strike than it does for the "advancing hand" to deliver the blow. This means that the return hand would be yang (active) and the advancing or striking hand would be yin (passive). Remember that all hand movements follow circular or round patterns. "All turning and bending is curved." (FWS, line 115)

## The Components of a Martial Arts System

One of the first things I tell my new students is: there are only four things you need to learn in any martial arts system: stance, blocks, strikes, and target areas. We learn rooting first because if you don't have a strong stance everything else you do will be weak and impotent. Blocking comes next, because if you can't block effectively, you may never get the opportunity to counterstrike your attacker. Students of Hwa Yu learn two or three different techniques for clearing their midline and blocking oncoming attacks. We focus on protecting the midline because that is where all the vital organs are. Whole-body motion is applied to all blocks and punches, because body unity is far more powerful than trying to move your arms independently of your torso. Even if an attack comes from the side, such as in the case of a roundhouse punch or a roundhouse kick, you would defend it by turning your midline in the direction of the attack. Students are also taught to block hits to their groin area by turning either one of their arms or one of their knees into their midline. In regards to countering, the classification "strikes" is inclusive of any and all punches, kicks, throws, or restraints. Finally, students must learn about the target areas—the parts of the attacker's body most vulnerable to attack—in order to figure out how to most quickly disable their opponent.

"If the enemy retreats, stick with quick advance." (FWS, line 50) This principle is called "riding the wave." Often, upon realizing that his attack has been neutralized, your attacker may try to back off and regroup for another assault. But as he retreats, you should stick to him like glue and counterattack before he can recover. If you have remained centered and in control of yourself physically and mentally, this will be easy to do. From the Five-Word Song we learn, "When contact is made, the inner force comes forth at once. This gives no opportunity for the opponent to escape." (FWS, lines 93 & 94)

## How the Hwa Yu Student Is Naturally Prepared for Attack

A student of Hwa Yu should be prepared for a possible attack at all times, first by learning to maintain a calm, clear and alert mind, and secondly, by always keeping his or her body weight clearly distinguished between one or the other leg. At any given time, one leg bears or supports a larger percentage of the body's weight than the other does allowing for quicker reaction time than could be achieved by standing in a "double-weighted" stance (when the body's weight is distributed evenly between both legs). A double-weighted stance is referred to as a neutral or "50/50" stance. We call this stance neutral because, inevitably, we must begin somewhere, and so our forms begin in a neutral stance. However, like the neutral gear in a car you can only begin and end in a neutral stance: it is never used for self-defense purposes.

Lastly, it's important to heed this piece of advice from the Five-Word Song: "If one does not practice regularly, do not face the enemy." (FWS, line 22) All good things take time, so you can't expect to properly fend off a strong attack after just a few lessons. It takes many hours of dedicated practice to become adept at Hwa Yu. A 105-pound student is not going to defeat a 280-pound attacker after just a few classes. Practice consistently, and practice hard—and know that while you're practicing, you're improving your overall health and well-being.

## The Forms

Many of the verses in the Five-Word Song refer specifically to the practice of the Hwa Yu forms, providing us with the necessary tools for their correct performance. Within the Five-Word Song are all the rules needed for developing the correct body structure and type of movement required for us to be successful in our practice of Hwa Yu. It is also necessary for students of Hwa Yu to thoroughly understand the

Six Combinations and Eight Methods (see Chapter 3), whose principles equip us with tools needed to achieve whole-body unity.

The ultimate goal of a Hwa Yu student is to master the forms to the point of perfection, because this pursuit is the way by which you gain the maximum health benefits and the spiritual harmony the art offers. John Li would often comment to his students, "Practice every day until you can do it perfectly." Students must be patient and learn to move slowly and smoothly, which is the t'ai chi way. Each student's movements will gradually become smoother and more even as he or she progresses. This is a natural manifestation brought about through regular and continued practice. Additionally, as each student progresses, her breath will start to synchronize with her movements. This process will and must occur naturally. In the beginning, new students are told to breathe like a bellows. This means to fully expand the chest when inhaling and compress it when exhaling. This is a good rule of thumb as long as these breaths and chest movements are natural and not forced—breathe lightly. When the breath and movements have joined together naturally, they first aid one another, and then combine to move the chi. Interruptions or unevenness in one's breathing will cause blocks in that person's chi flow, which would be detrimental rather than helpful to one's overall health.

In the beginning, you should focus on the correct execution of each movement in the form and not on its self-defense application. Practicing with fighting in mind will inhibit you and make it difficult for you to obtain the calmness needed to perform the movements smoothly and precisely enough to fully develop your chi. I am not against discussing the self-defense applications of a movement with a new student, as I find that learning the application of a particular movement sometimes helps a new student to better understand the nuances of how the movement should be executed; that said, once the student understands the movement, all thoughts of fighting should be put aside until he or she reaches a more advanced level of training.

Does this mean that a first-level student may never acquire the ability to defend him or herself? Absolutely not. I could pass on a number of stories about Hwa Yu students who were able to repel or evade an attacker. One such story is about a young lady who had been studying with John Li at his Boston studio for a couple of years. One morning, upon entering the studio, she ran up to Li and gave him a hug and adamantly thanked him. Li stared at her, slightly puzzled, wondering why she was thanking him before class had even begun. She explained that on her way to class that morning she had been jumped by a couple of men who intended to mug her. She went on to say that although she had no idea of what she did, or exactly how she did it, she was able to send the attackers flying away every time they tried to grab her or her purse, until eventually they gave up and she was able to run away. The explanation for this is that even though she was unaware of it, her body had naturalized the skills of centering and balance, which enabled her to easily unbalance and ward off her attackers, who, fortunately for her, did not have these skills. Adhering to the laws detailed by the Eight Methods while practicing your forms will produce this amazing ability, which often goes unnoticed until it is needed.

A similar story involves an old friend of mine from college, to whom I had taught Hwa Yu over a period of several years. While traveling to China from England, my friend and her companion had scheduled a brief stopover in Budapest, Hungary. At one point during this layover, they were riding on a tour bus, which, as it turned out, was being worked by a band of thieves. Because the bus was very crowded, my friend was forced to stand for the duration of the ride. Once the bus started moving, one of the thieves tried repeatedly to strip her of her valuables, the bus lurched through a series of quick stops and starts. Luckily, my friend was able to ward off her attacker by maintaining her rooting and clearing her center as the thief repeatedly grabbed at her purse and backpack. Eventually, her attacker threw up his hands in frustration, and gave up his quest. Many of the other passengers, including her companion, did not fare as well, having been relieved of their wallets and other valuables. The point of these stories is that you should enjoy practicing your forms without focusing too much on fighting, as the self-defense skills will likely be there for you when you need them.

The Hwa Yu forms should always be practiced slowly, smoothly, and evenly. The more advanced a student is the slower they can practice their movements, however, in the beginning you just try to go slow and easy. If you try to go too slow in the beginning, you will likely get bored with your practice and may not have the motivation to continue.

Remember to stay rooted and keep the soles of your feet firmly planted on the ground at all times. John Li would always remind his students to keep their legs bowed, their shoulders low, and their arms and back round. While practicing Hwa Yu it is also essential to breathe naturally and continuously from the tan t'ien. Remember that interrupting or holding the breath while doing the form is very detrimental. Concentrate on keeping the buttocks muscles tucked under and on lifting up the crown of your head, which stretches the spine and raises the spirit. In order to feel the chi, one should concentrate on stretching his or her fingers from the end of the hand to the fingertips; stretch the fingers, but at the same time, keep your hands relaxed. This should produce a sensation of "pins and needles" within the palms, which is the beginning of chi—though certainly not its end. As your training progresses, the tingling will be replaced by a force that feels like a magnetic pull; next, the energy will pulse throughout the whole body, initiating a feeling of incredible lightness and elation.

A key element of Hwa Yu is the synchronization of the hands, which remain in close proximity to each other at all times. The hands also work in close coordination with the midline of the body. An adduction (movement toward the midline) is far stronger than an abduction (movement away from the midline), therefore, in Hwa Yu the hands always move along or toward the midline.

If a student truly wishes to progress in the study of Hwa Yu then he must stop all trivial thoughts and fully concentrate on his practice until he is finished. It is not simply practice that helps one improve his or her skills but rather perfect practice. Whenever John Li practiced Push Hands exercise with a new student he would find an opening right away and give the student a light slap. He would then admonish the student by saying, "You must concentrate from the very beginning to the very end."

The last thing to remember is to enjoy your practice and let it be fun. This exercise feels so wonderful, don't let it turn into drudgery; instead, you should feel its beauty and enjoy it as you would a nice walk on the beach.

## SOME RELEVANT VERSES FROM THE FIVE-WORD SONG

Line 20: *"The body should be straight in stance."* This verse means that the center axis of the torso should be vertical or plumb and the hips and shoulders are kept horizontal or squared. Also your shoulders should never lean in front of, or behind, your hips. Your head, shoulders, and hips all align on the same vertical plane. This will help you achieve optimal balance and your opponent will have difficulty finding an opening by which to attack you.

Line 44: *"All breathing shall be natural."* Never force your breath. You must learn to let it rise and fall naturally with your movement. This will smooth the chi, which is excellent for improving your health. When your chi is smoothed, the flow will increase, as will your ability to harness or direct it.

Line 8: *"The Taoists say, it is not one's will, but the will of nature."* Natural is a key word. If a movement doesn't feel natural it's probably incorrect. The first time I witnessed Hwa Yu T'ai Chi I was left speechless. I had never seen anything so elegant and graceful. It seemed so peaceful and serene yet, at the same time, I sensed an amazing power. This power comes from the fact that Hwa Yu follows the Tao, which the Chinese believe is the power source for and unifier of heaven, earth, and man. They further believe that t'ai chi and the Tao are one and the same, and that Yin and Yang is the power source that the Tao uses to manifest itself and propel the fluid movement of t'ai chi.

Line 39: *"Be calm as a resting Buddhist."* Remember the first verse "Empty the mind." It is important to let go of all thoughts and preconceived notions and to learn to be very calm, relaxed, and open to your present circumstances. You will not see the enemy's intent and ensuing attack if your whole being is consumed by countless thoughts of what might happen. The root of all fear is the unknown. Focus your mind and spirit only on what is real.

Line 40: *"Move as a dragon rising from hibernation."* Bend and stretch fluidly and carefully. Let all of your movements emanate from your center.

Line 51: *"The legs should be curved like a bow."* This creates peripheral balance to your stance and is essential to strong rooting. To accomplish this, you bow the upper thighs and knees outward. The knees should point in the same direction or line as the corresponding foot. The entire sole of the foot must be in contact with the floor or ground.

Line 52: *"While advancing or retreating, use force derived from the kidneys."* This statement refers to moving and turning from the waist. The kidneys rotate around the spine causing the waist to turn. John Li used to tell a joke whenever he was asked what belt he had. He would say, "I have a flesh belt." What he meant by this was that the area around his lower abdomen had become unusually flexible and strong through years of practicing.

Line 53: *"The arms and back should be round as if hugging."* Tuck your buttocks in and depress or hollow your chest. This will make your back appear rounded as if you were hugging a tree. As you hollow your chest remember to keep your shoulders hanging downward naturally; do not shrug your shoulders and do not pull them forward. Your arms should be curved or rounded at all times, with your elbows low or hanging downward slightly. You want to maintain a smooth curve in your elbows: don't bend them.

Line 54: *"Circulate your chi from inside to outside."* I like to call this "becoming one with your universe." You will feel as if you are part of the air around you rather than a separate entity placed within it. This feeling of lightness or serenity will create an awareness that will enable you to sense any negative or aggressive energy as soon as it invades your space. We've done experiments with this in our martial arts classes. One student would stand with his or her back to their attacker, and the attacker would then advance toward them while focusing all of their intent on the area of the defender's body that they aimed to strike. The object of this exercise was for the defender to feel or sense where his or her attacker intended to strike before any contact actually occurred. Almost all of the students were able to do this successfully. Some of the more advanced or senior students could sense their attacker's advance as soon as he or she made his or her first step.

Line 60: *"Your hands should be thirty percent to the front and seventy percent to the rear."* A simpler way of saying this is that the forward hand is yin (passive) and the rear or return hand is yang (dominant). The return hand is the one that starts the motion and drives the force into your root, which in turn creates the forward force for the forward hand. Because it is passive, or light, the forward hand will be able to generate the necessary speed to send your maximum power (thrust) forward.

Line 65: *"The idea of the movement is like a fierce tiger."* Your eyes direct your spirit. The eyes always precede the movements as if they were leading them. On the outside everything is concealed, but inside your coiled force is like a fierce tiger. You always appear calm and peaceful, but your spirit is always prepared for attack.

Line 66: *"The calmness of the chi is very gentle."* Because of this, your entire nature will change—you will become "softer" both physically and mentally. But remember, softer does not mean weaker. In fact, the opposite is true: softer is actually stronger. It is like water—as you try to move it, it cannot be moved. In this way, you will be much harder to throw off-balance or to control. Your movements will become extremely precise and controlled. You will step lightly and become far more surefooted than you ever were before. Often, when I enter a room someone will say, "Where did you come from?" This is because my movement is so quiet and soft that no one can hear me approach. And I don't have to purposely try to sneak up on other people—this happens when I am just walking normally.

Line 77: *"The idea of the movement seems not to move, achieving fluidness."* In the more advanced levels of training the form moves so very slowly that it is hard to tell that the practitioner is actually moving at all. To reach this level a student must first know the forms very well and then develop strong meditative skills. Also, when a student is able to move with extreme smoothness it will be difficult for an opponent to distinguish his or her movements. The opponent becomes in a sense hypnotized because all of the movements flow together seamlessly.

Line 97: *"All movement is balanced in circular fashion."* You move as if you were standing in a large sphere or a bubble that you do not want to puncture. Also remember the principal of "return" from the Eight Methods. This means that if something goes forward something must go back to counterbalance it. The same is true if something goes up—something must go down to counterbalance it.

Line 104: *"Movement of the legs and hands all work together."* Whenever you are Walking or taking a step, your hands continue to move while you are stepping. It is wrong to step first and then move your hands. Everything happens simultaneously.

Line 114: *"Bend and stretch fluidly."* In other words, relax all muscles and joints and don't be tense. Always direct any moving or stretching from your spirit.

Line 128: *"The mind (heart) should be empty; the abdomen should be solid."* You must empty your mind of thoughts and let go of your emotions by lowering everything, including your thoughts, to the tan t'ien, which is located in your lower abdomen two inches below the navel. This is one of the areas where the philosophies of Hwa Yu directly correspond to the I Ching (Book of Changes). The abdomen represents man, who sits in the middle between heaven and earth. The upper part of the body is like heaven and therefore is very light as if it was floating in the clouds. The abdomen is solid. The legs are grounded like the earth.

## FURTHER INSTRUCTIONS

The following pages contain photographs and illustrations of the first eleven sections of the Hwa Yu long form, as well as illustrations of one or more of the actual self-defense applications taken from each movement. In a few cases, I have omitted the self-defense application of a particular movement because it was either a repeat of an application that was already given or it was very similar to a previous application, or because it was simply too gruesome to show. All of the photographs that illustrate the form are labeled with an F followed by a number, such as F1, F2, F3, and so on. All of the photographs that illustrate the self-defense applications are labeled with the letters AP followed by a number, such as AP1, AP2, AP3, and so on. If a second application is illustrated for the same movement it is differentiated by the letter B, which appears after the number (e.g. AP1B). Note that you should not attempt to try any of these self-defense applications without a teacher's supervision.

Following the long form lessons I have included a demonstration of the Crane Form and some of its self-defense applications, and an explanation of Hwa Yu's fifteen Animal Forms. Photographs that illustrate the Crane Form are labeled CF1 for form, and CFAP1, indicating application.

In some cases the actual direction of the movements have been altered and turned to face the front in order to give the readers a better view of the hand positions. Where this has occurred I have added illustrations that show foot patterns to indicate exactly which direction you should be facing.

The following charts list the different movements or parts of the Hwa Yu long form. There are two charts, one for each half of the form. I have included instructions on how to perform what I consider to be the first five sections of the form. The sequences I have included here provide more than enough material to keep any student busy for some time. There are, of course, many more movements to learn; however, learning a few movements correctly is a lot more meaningful than learning a lot of movements superficially.

## Hwa Yu T'ai Chi Ch'uan: The Long Form, First Half

### Preparation

  A. Opening

  B. Beginning

### The Form

  1. Stop the Carriage and Inquire the Way (right)

  2. Stop the Horse at the Cliff (right)

  3. Close the Door and Push Out the Moon

  4. Scatter the Clouds and See the Sun

  5. Stop the Carriage and Inquire the Way (left)

  6. Stop the Horse at the Cliff (left)

  7. Pluck the Stars and Change the Dipper

  8. Wild Geese Flying in Pairs

  9. Close the Door and Push Out the Moon (different)

10. Lone Goose Leaves the Flock

11. Wild Horse Chases the Wind

12. Streams Flow Incessantly

13. The Crouching Tiger Listens to the Wind

14. Point East, Attack to the West

15. Green Dragon Stretches His Claws

16. Complete the Elixir in Nine Turns

17. Scatter the Clouds and See the Sun (different)

18. Push the Boat with the Current

19. Surround the Horse and Turn It Back

20. Flowers From the Vase Drop to the Ink Slab

21. High Mountain Flowing Water

22. Boy Presents the Book

23. Woodcutter Carries the Firewood

24. The Heavenly Ruler Points to the Sky

25. The Five Colored Clouds Hold Up the Sun

26. Support the Sky and Cover the Earth

27. The Swallow Skims the Water

28. Facing the Sun, Strike the Ears with the Fists

29. Intercept and Push with Both Hands

30. Gentle Breeze Sweeps the Lotus Leaves

31. Swallow Holds the Mud

32. Nimble Monkey Picks the Fruit

33. Fierce Tiger Turns His Head

## Hwa Yu T'ai Chi Ch'uan: The Long Form, Second Half

34. Circle Heaven and Earth

35. Wind Sweeps the Lotus Leaves

36. Press with the Hand and Punch

37. Guitar Hides the Face

38. The Falling Star Chases the Moon

39. Swallow Flies on a Slant

40. The Phoenix Faces the Sun

41. Overturn the River and Pour Out the Sea

42. Facing the Rear, Mount the Dragon

43. The Wild Cat Catches the Butterfly

44. Take Out the Beam and Replace the Pillar

45. The Wind Rolls Away the Scattered Clouds

46. The Hibernating Dragon Reveals Itself

47. The Black Dragon Flaps Its Tail

48. Equally, Observe the Autumn Beauty

49. While Passing on Horseback, Look at the Flowers

50. The Angel of Literature Offers the Dipper

51. The Swallow Flies Through the Clouds

52. Raise Your Hand to the Seven Stars

53. Wild Geese Flying in Formation

54. The Yellow Dragon Turns Its Body

55. Five Saints Visit the Kingdom of Heaven

56. The Lotus is Concealed Under the Leaves

57. The Phoenix Spreads its Wings

58. The White Crane Pecks the Food

59. The Moon Hangs On Top of the Pine Tree

60. Lift the Oxtail Upward

61. The Boy Carries the Lute

62. The Rhinoceros Watches the Moon

63. The Sparrow Hawk Flies Through the Forest

64. The Red Dragon Disturbs the Water

65. The Wind Moves the Duckweed

66. The Chi Rises to the Koulkun Mountain

67. Sink your Chi and Conclude Hwa Yu T'ai Chi

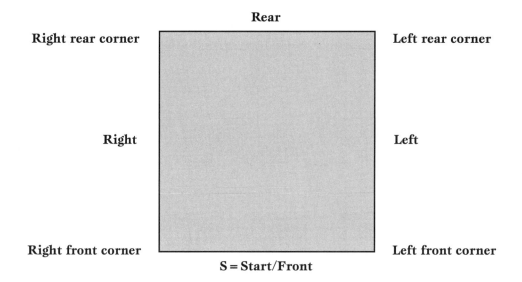

The above diagram is located underneath some of the photographs to indicate which direction that particular movement should face. S or Start refers to the first or beginning position, which will be our opening movement to the form. Any directions listed within the instructional sequences will always match the directions indicated in these diagrams. The line through the box (as shown here) indicates the direction your hips and shoulders should face.

You will constantly face different directions throughout the form, but the directions for the movements will always be given according to this chart. The footprints placed on the box, as shown below indicate the direction that your feet should face.

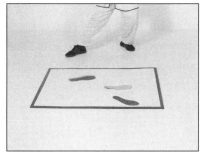

In some cases a box with footprints in it will appear either within the photograph itself, or it will be placed directly beneath the photograph. The light footprints show the foot placements from the previous move; the dark footprints show the new foot placements.

## *Section 1: Preparation*

F1             F2             F3

### OPENING

1. Figure F1 illustrates the starting position for the Hwa Yu long form. This posture is referred to as the neutral position (also known as the "50/50" or double-weighted stance). In this position the pelvis and tailbone are tucked just slightly and you sit into your hip flexors just a little so that you are comfortable. Your hands rest easily at your sides, adjacent to your upper thighs.

2. Figure F2 shows the first position of the Opening movement. The Opening is the first in a series of six movements that make up the Preparation section of the form. Start by rounding your arms and elbows and then moving them forward about six inches in front of your body. As your hands move forward, tuck your buttocks in and sit a little further into your hips. Remember: keep your feet pointing straight ahead, bow your legs, and hollow your chest.

3. In figure F3, I have raised my hands and arms upward, while keeping them connected as a single unit. They stop rising when they reach chin level. As you lift your arms, turn your palms upward so that they face the ceiling. When moving from position F2 to position F3, the hands emulate a scooping type of motion, much like scooping up a pile of leaves and lifting the pile upward. It's also necessary to round the arms and back even more and sit deeper into your hips as you raise your arms.

4. Figure F4 shows my hands at the top of their upward movement. They are now even with my eyebrows, and I have rotated my forearms so that my palms face one another. To do this, continue with the inward scooping motion until your hands reach your eyebrows. Then fan your hands outward—opening them up like a pair of wings—and stand up at the same time. (The hands start out as wide as your hips and scoop inward and upward until the two little fingers are nearly touching each other.) Continue sitting back and down into your hips as deep as you can until your hands reach your eyebrows, and then rise up as you fan the hands outward. Hollow your chest and stretch your arms out in the shape of a circle. Note that my fingers are stretching out and away from me.

  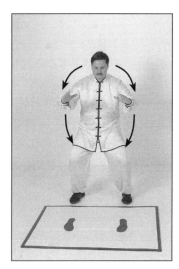

F4          F5          F6

5. Stand up until your knees are about ninety percent straight. Turn your palms outward slightly, so that they're facing one another; you should be able to gaze through them as if they were a pair of binoculars. From here your hands start to descend.

6. Figure F5 shows the arms and hands descending in a circular pattern. They should first circle out and then down in the shape of an oval or egg. You should also tuck in your pelvis and tailbone and sit back once again. As your arms sink down, your palms flatten out and face toward the floor. Photograph F6 shows me sitting in my lowest position, with my arms having descended to heart level.

7. Figure F7 shows the final position in the Opening movement. In this position, the hands continue down—holding the oval shape—as if they were pushing against something, such as a tabletop. As your hands push down, your body rises back up as if you were pushing yourself up. It's important to really stretch up the crown of your head in this position. Note the roundness in my arms—this roundness should be maintained until you are finished with the exercise.

F7

This completes the Opening movement to the long form. Now, we'll move on to a series of five movements known as the Beginning, which will complete the Preparation part of the form. Although it appears to be a rather simple movement, this Opening movement involves a tremendous amount of body mechanics and also contains a lot of valuable self-defense applications. From this movement a new student begins to learn the value of core or whole-body movement.

## OPENING: FIRST APPLICATION

AP1A

AP2A

AP3A

1. Figure AP1A depicts position F2 from the Opening. Karen Borla is defending, as I attempt to attack her with a bear hug. All she does is move her hands forward, forming a circle as I did in F2. As her hands move forward, she also sits back into her hip, which pushes my body back and away from her. With her arms in this rounded position I am left with nothing to grab on to.

2. Figure AP2A shows me attacking Karen with a front chokehold. She sits deep in her hips and scoops her arms up against the inside of my arms, just as I did in position F3 in the form demonstration.

AP4A

AP5A

3. In figure AP3A Karen has stood back up and opened her arms outward by expanding them into a large circle. She also turns her elbows out away from her midline by rounding them. Her hands have turned inward and now face one another. (This is shown in figure F4). The combination of her body rising and her arms rounding outward forces my hands to release her neck. It's important to note that while this is the quickest and most direct escape from a front chokehold, it will not work for a new student until they have practiced and learned the correct position of the arm joints and how to unite them with whole-body motion. There are other chokehold defenses from Yon Ch'uan (a sister art to Hwa Yu), as well as from other hard styles, that give a beginner more immediate success.

4. After Karen has forced me to release my grip, she sits back down into her hips once again while circling her arms and pushing her hands outward and then downward. She continues sitting down into her hips until her hands have sunk to her heart level (AP4A). This sitting motion would draw my body down and forward, giving her the option shown in figure AP5A: to raise her leg and counter my attack with a kick.

AP1B                          AP2B                          AP3B

## OPENING: SECOND APPLICATION

Master Robert Xavier (in black pants) demonstrates one of Hwa Yu's less compassionate self-defense techniques with his student John Phillips. As John attacks Master Xavier with a chokehold, Master Xavier raises his arms up and in-between John's arms while sitting back and down (AP1B & AP2B), just as we saw Karen do in illustrations AP2A & AP3A. But then Master Xavier rises back up and forward with his body and thrusts his hands out and forward at the same time, attacking John's face (AP3B). This technique would attack the eyes, ears, and nose of the assailant. The whole-body motion is achieved by driving the hips up and forward, which is what makes this counterattack so powerful. Master Xavier then adds insult to injury by sitting back down once again and drawing his assailant's body weight down and forward (AP4B). He finishes his defense by lifting his right knee into his attacker's chest (AP5B). This is a very fast and devastating defense that would render an attacker completely immobile.

The photograph (AP6B) illustrates a more compassionate option for this defensive skill. This time Master Xavier has chosen to employ a takedown—rather than take John's head off!

Please note that it takes considerable practice to execute this technique effectively. When Master Xavier photographed this series it was done in slow motion so that he could keep a safe distance from John's face. Neither he nor I would dare be foolhardy enough to practice this particular skill at full speed with a live partner. It is far too dangerous for that.

AP4B                    AP5B                    AP6B

## *Part 2: Beginning (Movements 1–4)*

1. Figures F8 and F9 demonstrate the first Beginning movement. This movement follows the Opening stage of the Preparation series; it is the first in a series of five movements. Note that the first two movements in this set are executed while standing in a double-weighted stance, as is the Opening. This means that your

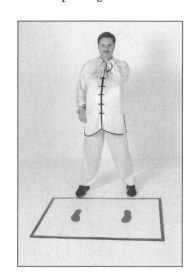

F8                              F9

weight is distributed evenly between your two legs. In figure F8 I have sat back into my hips once again and circled my left hand and arm inward to my centerline. As your hand moves to your centerline, rotate the palm clockwise, turning your thumb inward. In addition, turn your midline forty-five degrees toward your right front corner. (The knuckles of your left hand should be exactly on your midline. This means that your fingers would extend slightly past the midline.) As your left hand moves in, your right hand remains where it is, though the forearm should rotate, turning the palm outward. Remember to keep your elbows rounded and slightly back.

2. In figure F9, I first relax my left hand a little by letting it drop down, and then I lift my left wrist upward along my midline to the height of my nose. As you do this motion, draw your right hand back to the side of your right hip. (You should imagine that there is a balloon in your arms; as it fills with air, it forces your arms to move apart). At the same time that your hands are moving apart, your torso is rising back up and you should return your midline back to the front once again. This instills a whipping effect into the left wrist.

F10

F11

3. Figures F10 and F11 show the second Beginning movement. I start by sitting back into my hips once again (F10), and circling my left hand in and down along the

midline toward my heart, while my right hand circles forward and into my midline. The hands are now directly over one another, looking like a tiger's mouth.

4. To complete the movement I continue to circle my left hand in and down along my midline while circling my right hand up and out, with the fingers extended (F11). The middle finger of your right hand should end up on your midline and should be even with my eyebrows. As I raise my right hand, I also stand up, so that I am ninety-percent erect once again.

5. Next, let both hands rise up slightly and rotate to the right front corner by turning your torso forty-five degrees (F12). As your hands move to the side, turn your right palm outward. It's important to keep your hands on your midline and turn from your waist. Your hands should never move independently from the body. You should keep your center of gravity high (your knees should be ninety percent straight) as you turn, you should shift your weight back onto your left leg until it supports sixty percent of your total body weight.

6. In the next position, I sit back and down on into my left hip and press my hands downward to my heart level. Remember tuck in your tailbone and buttocks as you sit back, and follow along your midline with your hands (F13).

F12

F14

7. Continue to push your hands downward and raise your body weight up again. Once your hands are all the way down, sweep them back across to their starting point (F14). Your body weight is still supported mostly by your left leg until you complete your shift back.

8. In figure F15 I have returned to my starting position. To arrive back to this point, simply turn your midline back toward the front and slide your hands back into position with a sweeping motion (then separate them).

F15

## Application: Beginning (Movements 1–4)

AP6

AP7

AP8

1. In figures AP6 and AP7 Karen starts by turning her midline to her right front corner, while simultaneously circling her left hand inward to her center. This movement clears her centerline and wards off my punch to her solar plexus.

2. The next photo, AP7, shows her lifting her wrist to block my arm again as I alter my attack to go for her face. By turning her center back toward the front in a whiplike fashion, she has completely exposed all my vital target areas.

3. The final photo in this sequence, AP8, shows Karen drawing my striking arm down with her left hand and chopping into the glands under my chin with the outstretched fingers of her right hand. Her body rises up into the chop, which manifests the power for this strike. Her hands circle as if they were rolling a giant snowball. This is the application for the second Beginning movement (F10 & F11).

4. In photos AP9 & AP10, I am again attempting to strike Karen's face. She blocks my arm by clearing her midline (AP10) with a blocking technique that is taken from the second and third Beginning movements. Karen brings her hand upward in an arcing or circular motion, with the palm facing her. She then rotates the right palm outward toward her right front corner.

AP9                   AP10                  AP11

5. Next, Karen demonstrates the third Beginning movement by turning her hands and midline toward her right front corner and pushing out (AP11). This turning motion moves my center away from her into empty space. Instead of keeping her weight over her back leg as in the form, she advances by stepping forward,

sending me away as she pushes. The Hwa Yu form is full of hidden surprises such as this added feature, which is designed to give Karen the opportunity to run away at this point if she so desires. The blocking technique Karen uses in this defense skill significantly raises the attacker's center of gravity, which makes it very easy for a small person such as Karen to push away a person such as myself, who is quite a bit larger.

AP12

AP13

Figure AP 12 shows me attacking with a left punch to Karen's midsection or ribs. She breaks my balance by sinking and pressing down with her hands as in the fourth Beginning movement. She follows through by turning her midline back toward the front and sweeping her hands across to her left. By adding a slight turn of her right palm she locks my elbow, utilizing an armbar (a technique where the defender employs an elbow and/or shoulder lock on the attacking arm) to help her easily move me out of her space (AP13). In order to make this technique effective, Karen's arms and hips need to move in a circling motion, similar to what we did in Rowing, scooping downward and then upward. See the diagram below.

## BEGINNING (MOVEMENT 5)

F16

F 17

1. Figures F16 and F17 show the final Preparation movement. Begin by sitting back into your right hip, remembering to tuck the buttocks and tailbone under as we learned in rooting. Your body weight should be distributed as sixty percent on your right leg and forty percent on your left leg. Your midline turns forty-five degrees toward your left front corner. Your hands move forward in the direction of the left front corner, as if you were pitching a ball to someone using an underhand toss. Note that the hands are almost vertical, and facing one another (F16).

2. Continue lifting your hands upward until they reach the level of your chest (F17). As your hands rise up, raise your body weight and center of gravity by standing up on your right leg. Your body weight should remain 60/40 with most of the weight supported by the right leg; in other words, don't move your center of gravity forward as you rise up. We have now completed the Preparation part of the form, and are ready to start the first movement, Stop the Carriage and Inquire the Way.

## *Section 2: Parts 1–6 of The Long Form*

### PART 1: STOP THE CARRIAGE AND INQUIRE THE WAY (RIGHT)

**Stop the Carriage**

F18

F19

1. Starting from the last position of Beginning Movement 5, your right hand turns outward, opening a little, then comes down to your right hip as if you were swimming the crawl stroke (F18 & F19). Your right heel slides back forty-five degrees (keep the weight on the toes as your foot turns), and the toes of your left foot slide or turn to the left ending up at a ninety-degree angle. Keep the weight on the left heel as you turn the left toes to the front. Your midline has now turned ninety degrees to the left, from your starting direction. Your left hand will follow your centerline as it turns to the left, and as you turn, your left palm rotates out, turning down toward the floor (like skimming the surface of a pond or petting a cat).

2. Next, drop your left hand so that the fingers hang, or droop, down and your wrist is raised up (F20). Rotate your right hand until the palm faces up toward the ceiling; keep your right hand in contact with your right hip as it turns. Sit back into your right hip—this will lower your center of gravity. As you sit back, press

downward with the underside of the left wrist; your arm should feel as if there is a weight attached to your left elbow, pulling it down. The Five-Word Song states, "In this exercise all valuable points are concealed." (FWS, line 82) This means that you don't physically lower or move your hand down by itself. The downward motion is executed by sinking into the right hip and lowering your center of gravity, which will lower your hand with the use of whole-body motion, creating a much stronger downward pull than you would achieve by just using your arm.

F20                                F21

3. You complete this movement by standing, or rising, straight up on your right leg, while simultaneously chopping, or stabbing, upward with the fingers of your right hand (F21). Your right hand rises up on the inside of your left wrist until your middle finger is even with your eyebrows. (The middle finger should also end up right on your midline.) As you stand up on the right leg, let the left foot slide back toward your right foot until the left heel is even with the right toes.

## Stop the Carriage: Application

AP14           AP15           AP16

1. Photo AP14 shows Karen in a ready position and me preparing to attack with a straight right-hand punch to her midsection.

2. In photograph AP15, Karen has intercepted my punch with her left wrist and drawn me forward by sitting back and down into her right hip. Her left elbow is low in order to protect her ribs and abdomen, and her left hand has trapped my arm by draping over it. Notice that her right hand has prepared for her counterattack.

3. Photo AP16 shows Karen's counterstrike. She simply rises back up by straightening her right leg and hip, while thrusting the first two fingers of her right hand into the glands under my chin. The momentum of her whole body rising up into my oncoming force magnifies Karen's forward thrust, which means the faster I attack her, the harder I get hit.

## Inquire the Way

1. Photo F22 illustrates the first step of Inquire the Way. Starting from the last position in Stop the Carriage (F21), sit down once again into your right hip flexor (remember to tuck under). Then lower your hands while keeping them on your midline—first your left hand, then your right hand. Your right hand comes down slightly behind and above the left one, so that the tips of the fingers on the right hand are positioned just above the center of the left hand.

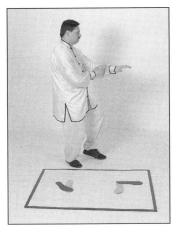
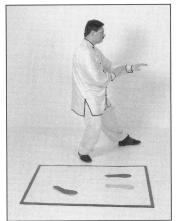

F22                     F23                        F24

2. Photo F23 shows me advancing my left foot into position. Advance the foot straight ahead and then step wider, just as we learned to do in Walking (see Chapter 5).

3. In the last photo in this series, F24, I am shifting my body weight down and forward, just as we learned to do in our Rowing exercise. As you move your body forward, draw your left hand back and advance your right hand forward at the same time. From the Five-Word Song we learn that the returning hand (the left in this case) moves back seventy percent and the right advances by thirty percent. As the right hand reaches its final position, raise the fingers up slightly, extending the right side of the palm. Your left hand should end up even with your right elbow. Remember to keep your arms and elbows rounded.

F25 Inquire the Way
(Front View)

## Inquire the Way: Application

AP17

AP18

AP19

1. Photo AP17 shows Karen posed in a defensive posture, with her weight supported mostly by her rear leg (by sixty percent), and me in attack position once again. This is for demonstration purposes only—a real attack would likely come without warning. But by supporting most of her weight on her rear leg, Karen is able to use her forward leg to either kick me or to step and evade my attack.

2. In photo AP18, Karen has sat back and down on her right hip, deflecting my forward attacking arm downward with her palms (she does this as she lets her body weight sink). Remember to tuck the tailbone and buttocks under as you sit.

3. Photo AP19 shows Karen's counterattack and the completion of the technique. First, she takes a Walking step, moving her left foot forward and wider, while still supporting her body weight with the rear leg. Next, as she rows forward onto her left foot, she parries or presses my attacking arm down and out slightly with her left hand while advancing and attacking over the top with her right hand. She has the option of striking me with either her fingers or the palm of her right hand. As she strikes me, she tucks under and sits down her front hip, utilizing the concept of return that we learned about from the Eight Methods (see Chapter 2).

## PART 2: STOP THE HORSE AT THE CLIFF

F26                F27

1. Stop the Horse at the Cliff starts where Inquire the Way leaves off (F24). Turn your left foot forty-five degrees to the left and turn the right foot, just slightly, away from your midline. Next, as you turn your midline to your left front corner, raise the fingers of your left hand up toward the ceiling and turn your right palm in so that it faces your left palm (F26). Imagine that you are holding a softball in your hands, and keep your body weight over the forward leg.

2. The final step of this movement is to raise your torso up and back, and then sit on your rear, or right, leg just as you would do in the Rowing exercise. As you sit back, lift your right hand up to your temple and let your left hand move down and then forward. You complete the movement by turning your midline slightly

to the right. The right hand also moves to the right using the whole-body motion you create as you turn your center. Keep the front (left) knee bent just a little. You never want to lock either knee (F27).

## Stop the Horse at the Cliff: Application

As I attack Karen with a left roundhouse punch (AP20), she clears her midline with her right arm, intercepting my attack. She then defuses my strike by sitting back and

down into her right hip, while simultaneously counterstriking with the outer edge of her left palm, into my solar plexus. Notice that as Karen sits back onto her right leg it causes her center-line to shift right. This pulls my body weight forward and downward onto my left leg, so that I end up falling into her counterattack. Essentially, she is using my body weight and momentum against me to such a degree that I am practically hitting myself. (Note that her feet are placed at a ninety-degree angle, with each pointing toward the opposite front corner).

AP20

## PART 3: CLOSE THE DOOR AND PUSH OUT THE MOON (5 MOVES)

F29

F30

F28

## Movements 1 & 2: Close the Door and Push Out the Moon (left side)

1. Figure F28 shows me rising up in my stance—with sixty percent of my weight supported by my back leg—and turning to my left front corner. As you turn, form an augmented block by placing the palm of your right hand against your left forearm. The two middle fingers of your right hand press in against the left wrist joint to support your left hand.

2. Next, circle your arms counterclockwise, turning them to the left and then downward. Using whole-body motion, turn at the waist by imaging that you are moving your kidneys around the base of your spine. Keep your hands on your midline throughout the entire turn (F29). This move is Close the Door.

3. Once your hands have completed a 180-degree rotation, step to your left front corner. This movement is called Push Out the Moon. Your left foot now points toward the corner, while your right heel slides back slightly (F30). Now, row down and forward, jabbing or chopping upward with the fingers on your left hand as you advance. Your weight should now be centered over the toes of your front leg. As you row forward and chop, you should tuck your pelvis under and forward and hollow in your chest. This action follows the return principle described in the Eight Methods. (see Chapter 3.)

AP21

AP22

AP23

AP24

AP25

## Close the Door and Push Out the Moon: Application

1. Photo AP21 shows Karen facing me once again in a defensive posture. Her weight is sixty percent on the rear leg and forty percent on the front leg.

2. In photos AP22 and AP25, Karen is utilizing the augment block from Close the Door. Because she is using the proper body alignment and employing whole-body unity to execute her block, she is able to successfully stop my attack, even though I am punching her with one of the strongest techniques in my arsenal. This augmented block is a very important maneuver for smaller individuals to master if they want to be successful in defending themselves against adversaries who are considerably larger.

3. In photo AP23, Karen has circled her hands, and her centerline, around to the left and down. This has drawn my body forward to my right front corner. This puts me off balance, which means that I no longer have control over my own center of gravity.

4. Because I have been drawn off-balance, I am now vulnerable to a counterattack, which is shown in photo AP24. Instead of utilizing the counterattack shown in the Push Out the Moon sequence of the form, Karen has opted to attack the side of my face with an ear slap meant to rupture my eardrum. (Of course, when practicing with each other, we don't actually push into the eardrum and cause injury.) This counterattack is more effective for beginners than the finger thrust because striking effectively with the fingers requires one to be able to draw on a considerable amount of chi and internal force.

5. Photo AP25 shows a close up view of the augmented block from a slightly different perspective.

## Movement 3: Play the Guitar

F31                F32                F33

1. The third movement in Close the Door and Push Out the Moon is called Play the Guitar. There are four steps to this sequence, which picks up from the end of Push the Moon. Step 1: Your left hand rotates clockwise forty-five degrees and sweeps inward from the rear left corner, which is where it now faces (F31). Its next position will be on your midline facing directly to the left of your starting direction. Step 2: Turn your hips and midline forty-five degrees to the right so they are also facing to the left of your starting point. (The little gray boxes in F31 indicate which direction your hips and feet should face). Step 3: Step your right foot forward,

just as we learned in the Walking section, advancing it along your centerline. As you step forward, drop your right hand down until it is positioned directly under your left hand. When you step, leave the right foot on the centerline—do not step wider, as you would in a normal Walking step (F32).

2. For the final segment, sit down into your rear (left) hip flexor, and circle your hands along your midline as you sit back. The left hand circles back and down, and the right hand circles up and forward (F33). Remember to tuck your buttocks in and sink your chest as you sit into your left hip flexor. (Although this movement was taught to me as Play the Guitar, I am almost certain that guitars as we know them today did not exist in 960AD. This leads me to believe one of two things: either this name was added later, or it is a modernized version of something like Play the Lute.

## Play the Guitar: Application

AP26

AP27

1. In photograph AP26 I am attacking Karen by attempting to grab her shirt. She wards off my attack by clearing her midline with an inside forearm block, using her left arm. Remember, this is how we began the movement Play the Guitar—by sweeping our left arm into our centerline. To complete this first phase of the movement, Karen steps forward with her right foot and drops her right hand under her left hand (both are on her centerline).

2. Karen finishes the technique by sitting back and down into her left hip and circling her hands vertically along her midline. Her left hand circles in and down, and makes contact against my lower forearm just above my wrist. At the same time, her right hand circles upward and she places it under the elbow of my attacking arm. As she sits back and down into her left hip, her left hand pushes down on my wrist and her right pushes up against my elbow, forming an armbar (AP 27). The Five-Word Song states that in the process of doing the form, "all valuable points are concealed." (FWS, line 82) The hidden gem in this movement lies at the very end of the technique. If Karen rotates both her hands clockwise as she completes her tuck, it greatly increases the leverage that she is able apply against my elbow joint, which will give her far better control over my body.

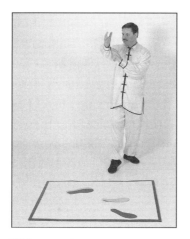

F34

F35

F36

F37

## Movements 4 & 5: Close the Door and Push Out the Moon (right side)

1. The final sequence in this series is to Close the Door and Push Out the Moon on the opposite side. (Note that the movement ends there; you do not repeat Play the Guitar.) Beginning from where we left off with Play the Guitar, we perform the same movement we did a moment ago but to the opposite or right side, instead of to our left as we did earlier. Stand up on your left leg and form an augmented block by placing the palm heel of the left hand alongside the right forearm (F34). Next, circle your right arm around and down, clockwise, and lower your weight by sitting into your left hip (F35). As you circle the arm, also rotate your midline along with it so that you employ whole-body motion. Your hand stays centered on your midline throughout the entire movement.

2. If you have circled your centerline and arms correctly, you should now be facing the left front corner (to the left of your starting position).. Step your right foot straight toward the left front corner (F36). Advance your body weight forward via a rowing motion (pushing down and forward) into your right leg, and stab or chop upward with the fingers of your right hand as you advance. (F37). The index and middle fingers are doing the striking in this exercise, and they should end up even with the bridge of your nose. Again, your target is the area right under the opponent's jawbone; in a life-or-death fight, you would strike with enough force to penetrate four inches.

### PART 6: SCATTER THE CLOUDS AND SEE THE SUN (2 MOVES)

F38

F39

F40

F41

1. Photo F38 shows me starting the movement by sweeping my right arm across to my left in an arcing motion, and at the same time turning my hips and midline forty-five degrees to the left. This inward movement of the right arm is an inside forearm block. Next, I sit back and down into my left hip flexor. As I sit back, I raise my left arm slightly and turn my right arm down and out toward the right, slightly, in an arcing or circular motion (F39). This completes Scatter the Clouds.

2. For the second part of the movement, See the Sun, I advance by rowing downward and forward, and as I am moving forward I sweep my left arm into my center and down, forming a half circle. After my left hand drops below my right arm, I rotate my right palm inward and raise it up slightly so that it ends up even with my midline, just below eye level (F40 & F41).

## Scatter the Clouds and See the Sun: Application

AP28

AP29

1. Scatter the Clouds begins with Karen intercepting my left jab with an inside forearm block, using her right arm (AP28). As I continue to attack her with a right roundhouse punch, she sweeps my left hand out of the way by turning her right hand down and out, while simultaneously clearing her center with her left arm—which then turns outward to her left, neutralizing my second attack (AP29).

2. Illustrations AP30 and AP31 show the second movement in this defense, See the Sun. As I kick Karen with my right leg, she sits deep into her left hip and blocks the attack by sweeping her left arm in to her center, then down. The instant she has deflected my kick, she rows forward and brings her right hand into her midline and upward, to slap my ear. This defense could easily rupture my eardrum. (Remember, when we practice these applications, we do not really hit each other.)

AP30

AP31

**PART 7: STOP THE CARRIAGE AND INQUIRE THE WAY (LEFT SIDE)**

F42

F43

1. Photographs F42 and F43 illustrate the movement Stop the Carriage, this time done on the left side. This movement is similar to Stop the Carriage right side, which was the first movement in the form after the Preparation. This time, instead of raising your center up into the finger chop, you will simply shift your body weight back and down as you strike. Beginning from your last position, See the Sun, drape your right hand downward without changing your arm position. If you have done this correctly your right wrist will be raised up and your right hand will drape downward. Now rotate your left forearm and turn your left palm upward so that it faces the ceiling. Your weight remains sixty percent on the forward (right) leg. Rise up and move your body weight back onto your rear (left) leg employing a rowing motion. Sit back and down on your rear leg, and chop or stab upward with the first two fingers of your left hand as you tuck and sit (F43). Both your right wrist and the first two fingers of your left hand should now be aligned on your midline. This concludes the movement Stop the Carriage.

2. For the next movement, Inquire the Way (F44 & F45), keep your body weight supported by your left or rear leg and tuck your pelvis in a little more. As you tuck, turn the fingers of your right hand outward so that they are pointing straight ahead along your midline. Lower the right hand into position just below your diaphragm. Now, lower the left hand on top of and slightly behind your right hand. The middle fingers of both hands should be aligned and centered on your midline. Move your body weight forward onto your right leg by rowing down and forward. As you row forward, draw your right hand back slightly and push your left hand forward. As your hands move apart, they remain aligned on your midline and your fingers remain pointed upward slightly. Once your body weight is over your front leg, tuck in your pelvis and sit into your front hip flexor. As you complete this tuck, raise the fingers of your left hand and push the left palm forward. Turn your hand slightly so that you strike with the bone on the outside of the left palm.

F44                              F45

## PART 8: STOP THE HORSE AT THE CLIFF (RIGHT SIDE)

F46

F47

1. Stop the Horse at the Cliff (right side) is performed in the opposite sequence of Stop the Horse at the Cliff (left side). Starting from the end of Inquire the Way, turn your right foot outward forty-five degrees so that it points toward the left front corner (note the foot diagram under photo F47). Turn the toes of your left foot outward, slightly away from your midline. Rotate your left forearm and palm inward until they face you. Then lift the right hand and point the left fingers straight upward while turning the palm inward slightly (F46).

2. Rise up and sit back onto your rear leg using a rowing motion. As you sit back and down onto the left leg, let your left arm rise up slightly while pushing your right hand and arm forward toward the left front corner. This striking motion is similar to the Rowing pattern, down and forward in an elliptical movement. Your midline should turn slightly to the left so that it faces the left side (F47).

Master Xavier in a position from Streams Flow Incessantly.

# ~7~

# The Hwa Yu Long Form: Sections Three, Four, and Five

The first two sections of the form are designed specifically to help new students to train and develop their hip flexors. If you take a close look at the movements, you'll notice that there are a lot of deep hip sits, which were put into the exercises just for that purpose. You'll notice in these next few sections that we begin to walk more. The first movements were more or less stationary with basic up-and-down motion. Then we added spiraling, or turning of the arms and spine, followed by shifting our body weight, first from side to side, then back to front. Now, we're going to add Walking in conjunction with these skills.

As you can see, there is a pattern developing; each series of movements gets more and more complex and intricate. The Hwa Yu long form is a step-by-step sequence of movement development and neuromuscular training. For this reason, it's important to fully learn and master each series of movements before going on to the next set. If you learn a lot of movements without taking the proper amount of time to understand the underlying concepts, you'll have wasted your time.

Once again, I would like to remind you that you should not attempt to execute the applications without a trained instructor present to make sure that you do them safely and correctly. These illustrations are included mainly to help you better understand how to perform the movements you learn in class.

F48

F49

F50

F51

## *Section Three*

### PART 7: PLUCK THE STARS AND CHANGE THE DIPPER

## Movement 1: Pluck the Stars

1. Pluck the Stars begins from the last position of Stop the Horse at the Cliff (right side). Move your body weight forward onto your right leg with a Rowing motion, and bring your left hand inward toward your midline so that it ends up mirroring

your right hand, with the palms facing one another in the Hold the Ball position. Point the fingers of both hands up toward the ceiling (F48). As you move forward, lift your left heel and then rotate it toward the rear right corner. This will enable you to rotate your hips around so that they face the left front corner (forty-five degrees from your starting point).

2. Step your left foot up to your right foot and stand up. When you step up with your left foot, place the heel close to the right heel and point the toes of both feet outward approximately forty-five degrees (F49). Although this stance is not as stable as most of the others used in Hwa Yu, it is necessary in this case because it allows you to get the proper spine and hip rotation needed for second part of the movement.

3. Tuck your buttocks in and sit very low; bow your knees as you sit and circle your arms and hands outward and downward. Continue the circle until your hands meet in front of your groin area. Bring your right hand inside your left and cross them at the wrists (F50 & F51).

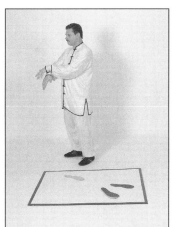 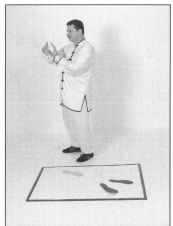 

F52                    F53                    F54

4. Stand back up and lift your arms upward along your midline. As you raise your arms, lift them up from the top of your wrists (F52). Your hands should continue to rise until they are just below eye level. Remember to employ the principle of whole-body unity and lift your arms and hands as a single unit. As you lift the arms and hands allow the elbows to drop slightly as if they had weights underneath

them, pulling them downward. Once your hands are lifted up to your face, turn or rotate the palm of your right hand so that the palm faces you. Circle your left hand over and behind the right hand, and then push your left middle finger against the joint between your right wrist and hand (F53).

5. Sit back and down once again, tucking your buttocks in and hollowing your chest as you do so. (Remember to bow your knees out.) As you sit back, push the back of your right hand forward as if you are striking an imaginary opponent in the nose. As you strike with your right hand, your left hand augments the attack by pushing outward against the right wrist (F54).

6. Rotate your arms and hands down and around counterclockwise 360 degrees, and as the hands start their ascent stand up once again—as your hands go up, your body goes up, too. As you rotate and stand, keep your hands on your midline and turn, as a single unit, from your waist. The axis of your turn is your tan t'ien and the base of your spine. As your hands move into their final position in front of your face, turn both palms outward. Your left hand falls in place first, followed by your right hand. The middle fingers of each hand should be aligned with your center (F54).

7. Sit down and back again; as you sit, pull your hands inward and then press them downward, following your midline the whole way (F55 & F56). Concentrate on your palms—imagine that they have weights in them. If you were actually in a fight, you would use this move to rake down your opponent's centerline (at the face and chest) with your fingers.

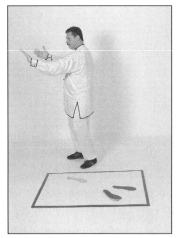

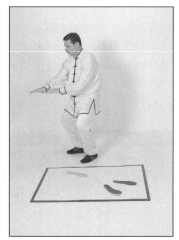

F55

F56

F57

## Movement 2: Change the Dipper

Stand up and separate your hands as if you are skimming the surface of a pond. You will still be facing the left front corner. Your hands are now in the same position as they were in the very beginning of the long form (F1).

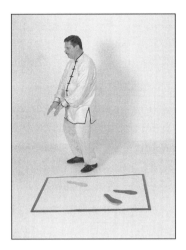

F58

## Pluck the Stars and Change the Dipper: Application

AP32

AP33

AP34

1. As John tries to grab me, I form my arms into the Hold the Ball position and let them rise upward, slipping them in between his arms as he attacks (AP32). With my hands in this position, my arms form a protective shield that keeps his attack outside of my reachable space. Note that you must keep your elbows and arms nice and round for this move to be effective.

2. I now bring my rear foot forward and stand up (AP33). My advance will push John's body weight back a little, giving me room for my next move, which is to circle my arms out, around, and down (AP34 & AP35), which traps John's arms and forces them down.

3. Next, I bring my hands together—with the right hand moving behind the left— and then lift them upward from the wrists, to my face. Note that I keep both wrists on my centerline as I raise them (AP36). The back of my right hand is facing John; my left hand circles over and behind my right hand. I sit back and down into my root while counterattacking John with the back of my right hand, using a quick slapping motion. This slapping technique is augmented by my left hand, which pushes out against my right wrist as I strike (AP37).

AP35                    AP36                    AP37

AP38                                  AP39

4. Even if John is lucky enough to evade my first counterattack by, say, moving his head back, (AP37), there are two more very quick attacks waiting for him (AP38 & AP39). First, I keep my left hand pressing against my right wrist, and circle both hands down, then bring them around and up. As I stand up, I bring my hands up and strike first with my left hand (with the palm), then quickly rotate my centerline back and strike with my right hand (AP39).

F59                        F60                              F61

## PART 8: WILD GEESE FLYING IN PAIRS

Wild Geese Flying in Pairs is the longest single section in the entire Hwa Yu long form. If you look closely at this movement, you can easily see how it got its name. In Wild Geese, you can actually see the hands moving together like a pair of flying geese. We will begin from the end of Change the Dipper. (Note that unlike Pluck the Stars and Change the Dipper, this sequence is shown in the direction that it occurs in the form).

1. Lift the heel of your right foot. Rotate your centerline and hips back to the front by turning on the toe of the right foot (F59). Then step your right foot toward the right front corner by executing a basic Walking step (F60). Row down and forward into your right hip and raise your arms up, following your midline. As you lift your arms, relax your hands and lift them up from the tops of your wrists, letting your elbows sink down a bit (F61).

2. Turn your midline toward the right front corner, while simultaneously circling your hands up and over toward the right front corner, using a clockwise motion. Roll your hands over by turning the palms up as they move to the corner. The left forearm rotates counterclockwise, while and the right arm spins clockwise (F62 & F63). Remember to keep your arms round and your elbows low.

3. Open your left foot by turning the toes to the left. Your feet should now form a right angle. This is known as an "L stance." Sit down into your right hip, and then shift back onto your left hip (F64 & F65). As you move back, pull as if you competing in a tug of war, and turn by rotating your midline ninety degrees to the left. Note that only your torso should do the turning: your hands should remain in their position and move only in relation to the torso (F65 & F66). Photograph F67 shows the hands rolled over, ready for the next movement.

F62       F63       F64

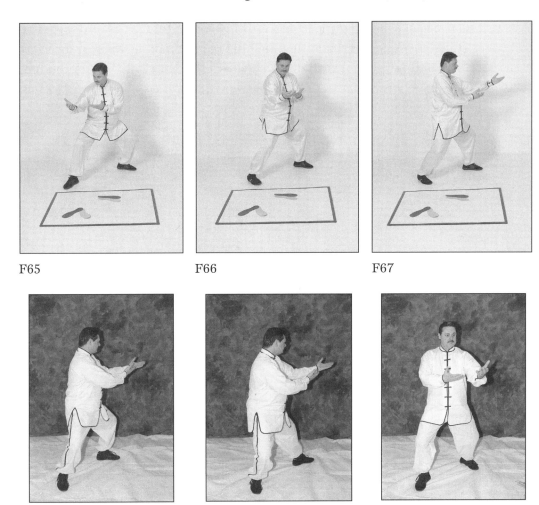

F65      F66      F67

F68      F69      F70

4. Continue the form by doing the same movement that you just did, but in reverse. Photograph F68 shows me sitting on my left (forward) leg, and F69 shows me sitting and pulling back as if I were competing in a tug of war. I finish the movement by turning my midline and torso forty-five degrees to the right, so that I end up facing my starting position (F70).

5. After you complete the turn, bring both hands to your midline at chest height, and arrange them into the Hold the Ball position (F70). Next, sit back and down into your left hip in Rowing fashion (F72). We finish this movement by turning our midline a quarter-turn to the left. Keep your hands aligned with your center

as you turn. Change your footing by first turning your right foot inward forty-five degrees (turning on the heel) and then turning the left foot outward in the same manner by rotating the toes forty-five degrees to the left (F73). When the foot turns on the heel (which moves the toes outward), it's called a "heel turn"; when the foot turns on the toes (which moves the heel) it's called a "toe turn."

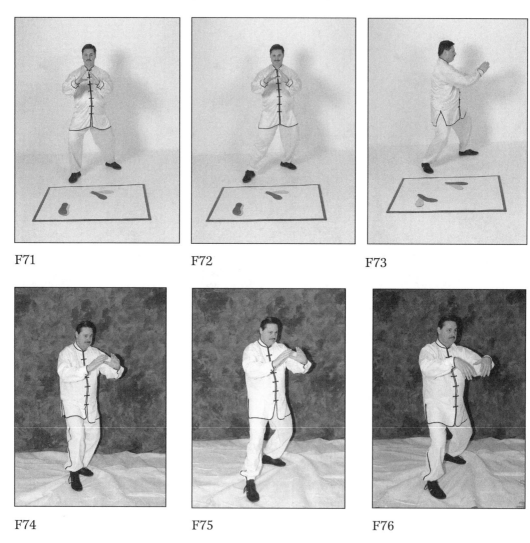

F71                    F72                    F73

F74                    F75                    F76

6. Step up with your right foot and rotate your midline and hips back to the right one-eighth of a turn, so that you end up facing your left front corner (F74). Continue to hold the imaginary ball with your hands, advance your right foot forward along

your midline, and then step wider as you learned to do in Walking (F75). Shift your weight forward by rowing down and forward onto your right leg. Let your center of gravity rise up slightly (stand up just a little on your front leg). As you lift your body upward, let your hands rise up and then drop over and down in a waterfall-like fashion (F76).

F77

F78

7. After your hands have rolled down and in, they immediately reverse, rolling up and back. This rolling back motion is executed as your body weight rows up, and then back, onto your rear leg. This creates a whole-body motion that resembles a wave. You finish off this pulling motion by sitting into your left hip (F77).

8. You complete this movement by rowing down and forward once again (F78). As you move forward, sweep both hands downward, along the midline and then open them outward, turning the Tiger's Mouth downward and outward as the hands separate. (Remember, the Tiger's Mouth is the space that's created when the thumb and index finger open up; refer to Photo S3 in Standing.)

9. Turn 180 degrees toward the opposite corner. (The photographs for this movement are shown in the opposite direction from which they actually appear in the form, so that you can see the hand positions. I should actually be heading 180 degrees in reverse, to rear right corner). As you turn, sweep both hands down and across at waist height. Turn the toes of your right foot inward using a heel turn, and then slide your left foot across to the left, so that its heel is in line with the heel of your right foot. Now sit back into your right hip and let your hands rise up along your

midline into a Play the Guitar position (F79). The left hand is forward and the right hand is held back (approximately even with the left elbow joint). This is an on-guard or ready position.

F79                    F80                    F81

10. Step forward with your right foot (F80), keeping it on your midline, and then sit back slightly into your left hip flexor. As you step, roll your hands so that the left hand circles up and back and the right moves down, forward, and then up so that your hands have reversed position. (In most cases, we keep the same hand and the same foot forward.)

11. Row your weight forward onto your right leg and step forward with your left foot. With your body weight still supported by your right leg, stand up so that you are about ninety percent erect. As you stand up, lift your right arm up above your head along your midline, and move your left hand up until it is at the height of your heart. Then push it forward and down in an arcing motion, like an arrow's path (F81).

12. You should have ended the last movement facing the right rear corner. That means that the next series of photos are shown in the same direction that they occur in the form. The first step (F82) is a simple reversal of the last move, with a 135-degree turn to the right. Turn to the right by executing two heel turns, one on each foot starting with the left. As you turn, reverse the position of your hands, lifting the left one above your head and dropping the right one downward

and outward. You can drop the fingers of the right hand forward and downward as we did in the last movement. Your body weight remains supported by the rear (left) leg. The right leg is light or empty. Turn your right foot to your right another ninety degrees, so that it is now facing your starting direction. This turn employs a heel turn, which can be easily done because the foot is empty. Keep your right hand on your centerline and let the hand drape down and point left (F83). Now drape your left hand over the top of your right in the same manner, pointing right.

F82

F83

F84

F85

F86

F87

13. Lift your left heel and rotate your midline and hips around to the front. You are now facing your starting direction. Turn slightly to your right and point the fingers and hands straight down, with the middle fingers of both hands in line with each other on your centerline (F84).

14. Turn your left knee so that it moves inside and behind your right knee (F85) and squat all the way down (without touching the floor). As you squat, keep your hands in the same line pointing down your midline and try to keep your back straight. This movement is rather difficult, so if you have trouble at first, it is perfectly fine to go only halfway down.

15. Turn your midline back toward your left front corner and stand back up. As you stand, lift your hands back up from the top of the wrists, while following your midline (F86 & F87).

F88  F89  F90

16. Facing your left front corner, pick up your left knee and lift your wrists at the same time. Keep both your wrists and your left knee aligned with your midline as you lift them (F88). Now, lower the left knee and sweep the left foot over slightly toward your left, pointing it to the left side of your starting direction (F89). Your hands will also continue to sink down along your midline as you do this, and then they'll separate so that each hand is aligned with its corresponding knee.

17. Move your body weight forward onto your left leg using a rowing motion. Once your weight is over the left leg, stand or rise up slightly while lifting both wrists, making sure to keep them aligned with their corresponding knees. As you lift your wrists, relax your hands and let them hang down (F90). To complete the movement, sit back down onto your forward leg so that your center, or tan t'ien, is lowered once again.

F91          F92          F93

18. Next, while sitting back onto your rear leg, circle your left hand and arm around to the left and down (F91). Then row forward once again and push up and forward with the outside of your left palm, as if you were pushing someone (F92).

19. You complete Wild Geese Flying in Pairs by repeating the previous movement on the opposite side. Row back onto your left leg while circling your right hand out and down in a clockwise pattern. Then push up and out while rowing forward onto your right leg (F93 & F94).

F94

AP40          AP41          AP42

## Wild Geese Flying in Pairs: First Application

As John reaches out to choke Master Xavier (AP40), Master Xavier clears his midline by raising both of his wrists first inward, then upward along his midline to block the attack. He then circles his hands clockwise and grips John's left arm both at the wrist and behind the elbow. This enables Master Xavier to apply an armbar (AP41). Master Xavier then sinks by sitting into his front leg, and pulls John forward and to his right (Master Xavier's left). Master Xavier then turns his midline to his left, which sends John away into empty space.

When doing this technique, it's important to keep both arms—as well as your opponent's arm, which you trapped in the elbow lock—aligned along your midline as you turn, thereby employing whole-body motion.

AP43          AP44          AP45

## Wild Geese Flying in Pairs: Second Application

This series begins with John attacking Master Xavier with his right arm (AP43). This attack could be either a punch or a grab. Master Xavier clears his midline by blocking the attack with a right inside forearm block. Master Xavier then grabs hold of John's wrist with his right hand, and locks John's elbow with the palm of his left hand (AP44). He then shifts his midline to his right while rowing his body weight forward onto his right leg. As he shifts his body, Master Xavier rolls John's elbow up, completing the arm lock. Master Xavier has now established control over his opponent. At this point, he has the option of continuing with the armbar and bringing John down onto the floor in a pin (as I

AP46

did in the corresponding form sequence F81–F84), or, as illustrated in photograph AP46, he can use a less compassionate approach. To execute this technique, Master Xavier must turn his centerline back inward, toward John, and then strike him by attacking upward with his knee.

## PART 9: CLOSE THE DOOR AND PUSH OUT THE MOON

F95

F96

F97

1. Though the name's the same, this Close the Door segment is different than the one in part three. First, bring your right hand inward to your right hip. As you bring the hand to your hip, turn it so that the palm faces up and the fingers point in toward the hip (F95). Now, let your right heel slide back, and rotate your hips and centerline to the left so that you are now facing the left side. Shift your weight forward onto the left leg. Drop your left hand down and position the left wrist on the centerline. Push or strike through with the outside edge of the right palm heel (F96).

2. Push Out the Moon is very similar to a movement that we did in Wild Geese Flying in Pairs. Sit back and then down into your right hip and roll your hands upward and then back toward your chest. As you roll your hands back, lift from the wrists then press down into your palms (F97). Then, as we did in Wild Geese, row forward and continue to press both hands downward, and then outward (F98). As you separate your hands, turn the Tiger's Mouth out. (Turn the opening between the thumb and index finger out toward the front.)

F98

F99

## PART 10: LONE GOOSE LEAVES THE FLOCK

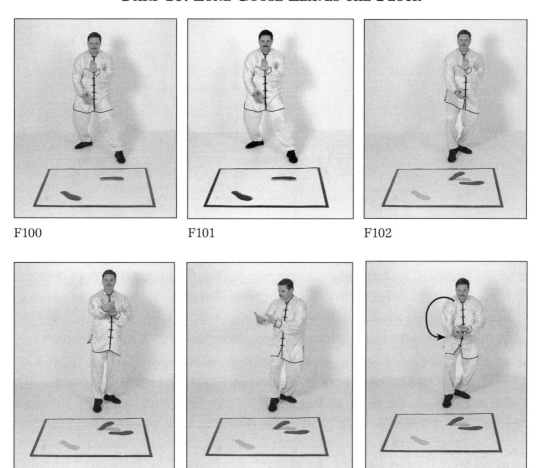

F100

F101

F102

F103

F104

F105

1. Sit back onto your right leg and circle your arms and hands. Both hands circle in a clockwise motion., but the left hand circles around and up while the right circles down and under. Both hands should end up on the midline directly above or below each other (F100 & F101). Row your body weight forward onto your left hip flexor. Once your weight is on your front leg, step forward with your right foot into the first Walking position (F103).

2. Chop upward with the right hand, and then circle both hands around to the right and downward (F103–F105). Keep your hands on your midline, and do all of the turning with your hips and waist.

F106                                    F107

3. Complete your Walking step by moving your right foot forward first, and then wider (F106). Row forward while chopping upward with the fingers of the right hand (F107). The left hand follows along with the right as it chops up. In an actual fighting situation the left hand would brace or augment the right wrist; however, in this situation, you simply imagine your chi supporting the opposite wrist.

4. We continue Lone Goose Leaves the Flock by performing the same movement once again, but in reverse (with the other side). Sit back into your left hip flexor and circle the hands as you sit back—this time, circle both of your hands counterclockwise. The right hand moves down, around, and up and the left arm circles around and down. Both of these circles occur simultaneously, as if the hands were turning on the same arc and remaining 180 degrees apart from one another (F108).

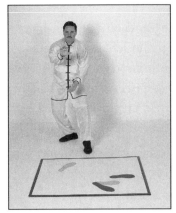

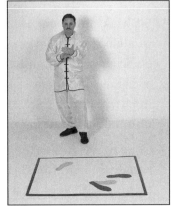

F108                      F109                      F110

5. Now, step forward with your left foot, into the first Walking position as shown in photo F109. Your hands simply hold their position as you step and your body weight stays low. After your forward step is completed stand on your rear (right) leg and thrust or chop upward with the fingers of your left hand as shown in illustration F110.

6. Both hands are positioned on your centerline at chin level, with the fingers of your right hand pointing toward your left wrist. Circle both arms together. Turn to your left and downward counterclockwise 180 degrees. (F111 & F112).

7. Finish your Walking step by advancing your left foot forward and then moving it wider. After the left foot is in place, row forward onto it while chopping upward with the fingers of your left hand. As you did in the last movement, keep your right hand pointed at your left wrist (F113).

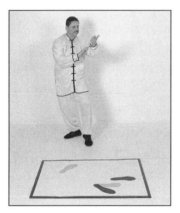
F111

F112

F113

F114

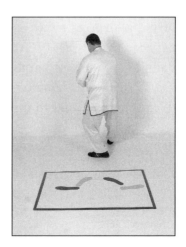
F115

8. Row backward onto your right hip and turn your left hand over so that the left palm faces the floor. Imagine that you are pressing down with your left palm as you sit back. Your right hand moves inward as you row forward again, so that it is lined up directly behind the left hand. Both hands point upward at a slight angle (F114). Open your left foot by turning it away from your center by forty-five degrees, and step your right foot forward, placing the heel down first (F115). As the right foot steps forward, let the right hand thrust forward and out, chopping forward over the top of the left hand.

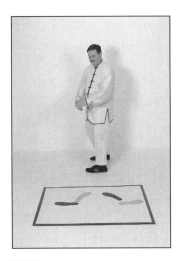

F116

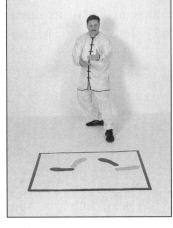

F117

9. Point the fingers off your right hand down, and rotate your left palm so that it faces the ceiling. Now, imagine that you are holding a very large ball in your hands. Turn 180 degrees by executing two heel turns, first with your right foot and then with your left (F116). After you complete your turn, sit back into your right hip and turn your left hand so that the fingers point away from you. The fingers of your right hand should now be pointing at the fingers of your left hand (F117). (We sometimes refer to this movement as Shoveling Coal).

## Lone Goose Leaves the Flock: Application

AP47                    AP48                    AP49

1. In illustration AP47, Master Xavier intercepts John's right arm with a left inside forearm block. After Master Xavier intercepts the attacking arm, he sits back and turns his midline just a little toward his right, so that John's attack is lead it into empty space. Master Xavier then rows forward and clears his midline with his right arm so that John's attacking arm is now positioned toward Master Xavier's front right corner. John is now quartered (AP48).

2. Master Xavier then steps forward into the first Walking position and circles his midline while turning his arms to the right and down (AP49). As you can see in the illustration, this places John off-center.

3. To complete the technique, Master Xavier finishes his Walking step by advancing his right foot forward and then moving it wider. He then rows forward onto his right foot while chopping upward with the fingers of his right hand into the glands under John's chin (AP50). If Master Xavier wanted to use a more compassionate approach, he could simply push John backward out of his reachable space, rather than strike him with the finger thrust.

AP50

## PART 11: WILD HORSE CHASES THE WIND

F118                    F119                    F120

1. Start from the final position of Lone Goose Leaves the Flock (F118). Rotate your left hand into a pressing-down position by turning the fingers inward and then dropping them (your wrist should be up, your fingers draped down). Row down and forward and chop up with the fingers of your right hand (F119). It's important to keep everything rounded—arms, elbows, back, and legs.

2. Raise your right hand up slightly and turn the palm inward so that it is facing you. Drop the left hand and turn that palm inward, too. Your hands should form a corkscrewlike shape. This protects both the upper and lower quadrants of your torso, like a shield, as you turn. Turn your left toes inward toward your midline using a heel turn. Keep your body weight supported by your left leg as you turn; do not shift forward yet. As the foot turns, your midline should also begin to rotate. Now, turn your right foot out ninety degrees (away from your midline), and shift or row your weight forward onto the right leg (F120 & F121). Your left foot is now light, so step it forward, setting its heel down in line and ahead of your right heel (F121). To finish the movement (F122), turn your left toes in, using a heel turn, and turn your midline back around to the front. (This sequence is shown in its actual direction).

Turn both palms out to the front, and arrange your hands over one another to form the Tiger's Mouth. (This Tiger's Mouth is different than the one formed in the hands with the thumb and index finger.) Sit back into both hip flexors and push both of your palms forward, opening them up as they press forward. This movement requires you to push forward while sitting back, a skill that requires a high degree of mastery in the Eight Methods' principle of return, as well as superior rooting skills.

F121                     F122

The entire Wild Horse movement then repeats itself on the other side, however, we're going to conclude our form instruction at this point. I have provided enough material to keep anyone busy for more than a year.

## Wild Horse Chases the Wind: Application

In photograph AP51, John is grabbing Master Xavier from behind and attempting to wheel him around to deliver a punch. To protect himself, Master Xavier clears his upper and lower quadrants with a spiral-, or corkscrew-, type blocking formation; this will protect him no matter if the punch is aimed high toward his face or low toward his torso. As John pulls Master Xavier from behind, Master Xavier slides his right foot back and over to the left, stepping in between his left leg and John's forward leg (AP52). Once his foot is in position, he turns to the right and faces his attacker. As he turns, he first clears John's grabbing arm, then forms his hands into the Tiger's Mouth position. He completes the technique by sitting back into his hips and thrusting forward with his hands to counterattack John. Master Xavier's upper hand attacks John's neck, while his lower hand strikes John's groin (AP53).

AP51           AP52           AP53

A posture from Wild Geese Flying in Pairs.

# ~8~

# The Animal Forms and Push Hands

Once new students have developed their rooting ability to a satisfactory level, they begin to study the Animal Forms in conjunction with learning the first few sections of the long form. Initially, Chen Hsi-I created twelve short forms in this set, each one mimicking a different animal. Master Robert Xavier added three others to the list about ten years ago to bring the total to fifteen. Each of the fifteen animal movements can be found within Hwa Yu's long form.

The Animal Forms were developed in order to isolate some of the important fundamental skills that beginners need to learn, such as stance, stepping patterns, basic blocking, and whole-body movement. You can also draw a lot of self-defense knowledge from these forms, such as creating effective contact with your opponent (blocking or intercepting skills), quartering capabilities, and counterattacking knowledge.

Because these Animal Forms are short—each containing ten steps or less—new students are usually able to learn the basic skills and mark the movement patterns relatively easily. However, as with most martial arts systems, perfecting these movements will then require quite a lot of practice. Though the movement sequences are not overly difficult, don't make the mistake of thinking that these forms are either weak or a waste of time. Actually, these forms contain a tremendous amount of very sophisticated and effective fighting skills, which are useful for any student, whether a beginner or an advanced practitioner.

As an example of the Animal Forms and their self-defense capability, Master Xavier and John Phillips are shown performing the Crane Form, which is followed by a sequence of self-defense applications taken directly from that form.

## *The Crane Form*

1. Master Xavier and John Phillips start the form in a ready position, with their weight on their forward legs and their arms held in a neutral position (CF1).

2. From this neutral position, shift your weight to your rear leg and slide your right foot straight across until it lines up with the heel of your rear foot. As you slide your front foot across, execute an inside forearm block by circling your right hand upward along your midline (CF2).

3. The next two steps (CF3 & CF4) should be done as one movement. Open the toes of your right foot by executing a heel turn. Once the foot has turned, step through with your left foot to face toward your right front corner. As you step up, you perform a movement with your arms called Roll the Ball. Your right hand, which was raised up in the last movement, rotates so that the palms turn downward and then draw back and down in a circular motion. At the same time, the left or rear hand rotates so that the palm turns up, and it circles forward and up. It will appear as if the hands have simply switched positions.

4. In CF5, John and Master Xavier slide or step their left legs all the way across to the left until they are in a shoulder-width stance. They return their hands to the ready position.

5. Once you have reset in this stance, row forward onto your left leg while striking with the heel of your left hand (CF6).

6. Advance your right foot forward with a full Walking step. Then, as you shift your body weight forward onto your right foot, strike with your right elbow by bringing it up and over slightly, then down at an angle into your opponent's chest (CF7).

7. Now, row back onto your left leg again, and form a hook with the outside of your right wrist (CF8).

8. Step back with their right foot, and sit back while executing the Roll the Ball movement again (CF9). (We'll show you what this movement looks like in the application section.)

9. Lastly, row forward onto your left leg and strike forward into your opponent's chest with the heel of your right hand.

CF1

CF2

CF3

CF4

CF5

CF6

CF7

CF8

CF9

CF10

## THE CRANE FORM: APPLICATION

CFAP1

CFAP2

CFAP3

1. In illustration CFAP1, John is punching Master Xavier with a right jab (a straight punch). Master Xavier evades this attack by stepping across to his left with his right foot while executing an inside forearm block to the outside of John's right arm. We call this technique an "inside forearm block" because the hand spirals in and then upward along Master Xavier's midline.

2. Once he has made contact, Master Xavier then needs to gain control of his attacker. He accomplishes this by spiraling his right arm and hand out clockwise and grasping the top of John's wrist with a Tiger's Mouth grip. At the same time, he executes a Roll the Ball movement, which brings his left hand upward so that he can place it behind John's elbow to form an arm lock. Master Xavier then sits into his right hip while pulling down on John's attacking arm. This pulling-and-sitting motion will force John's body weight down and forward, which, of course, throws him off-balance (CFAP2).

3. In CFAP3, Master Xavier moves his right foot wider by stepping it straight across to his right so that his legs end up shoulder-width apart. Once the right foot is in place, he attempts to row forward and counterstrike John with the outer edge of his right palm. As you can see in the photograph, John has blocked this attempt by using an inward palm block. If Master Xavier were to follow the Crane Form sequence, he could continue his attack by lifting his right elbow up and over John's blocking arm, and then striking downward toward John's chest.

4. Illustration CFAP4 shows a new defensive technique. This series begins after the elbow strike that is seen in the form sequence (CF7). Master Xavier sits back into his left hip while hooking John's right arm. With his front leg now weightless or empty, Master Xavier can take a step back with his right foot. As he steps back, he executes the Roll the Ball movement once again and traps John's right arm in an armbar. John's arm is now trapped and Master Xavier can draw him off-balance by sitting into his rear leg (CFAP 5).

CFAP4                    CFAP5                    CFAP6

5. John's body is now too far off-balance for him to possibly recover. Master Xavier uses this opportunity to release his counterattack by striking John in the face with the heel of his hand. In order to practice this move safety, Master Xavier has struck to the side of John's face rather than actually hitting him. In the form, we saw John and Master Xavier execute this strike to the opponent's chest, however, we only use the forms as a guide to practice our skills—in a real-life fighting situation you must be able to read your opponent's movements and adjust your counterattack strategy instantly. In this scenario, John's body weight had been pulled so far forward by Master Xavier's sitting-and-pulling motion that going for his chest was no longer appropriate; therefore, Master Xavier adjusted his movement and attacked the target that was most exposed and vulnerable at that moment.

## *Push Hands*

PH1           PH2

The Push Hands exercises that are practiced in Hwa Yu are a lot more complex than the variations normally found in other systems of t'ai chi. We do use the basic Push Hands routines (push, press, draw, and roll back) found in other systems to help new students develop sensitivity to an opponent's balance and energy; however, this merely a starting point. Once students have become sensitive to their opponent's movements, and have learned to practice without the use of physical strength, every movement that is found within the Hwa Yu forms becomes a Push Hands exercise. We have a saying, "An attack is best defended by its own mirror image."

In the above photographs (PH1 & PH2) Master Robert Xavier and John Phillips are practicing a Push Hands exercise for the movement Scatter the Clouds and See the Sun. They can trade this movement for an indefinite amount of time, with first one person attacking and the other defending and vice-versa. Just about every movement in Hwa Yu can be practiced in this manner.

As students of Hwa Yu progress in their general training and learn the forms, they attack and defend using whichever movement from the long form that they feel is appropriate. Sometimes they may opt to practice using just their pushing and pulling techniques; at other times, they may practice using the full array of Hwa Yu's offensive and defensive skills. Remember, you establish light contact with your opponent's wrist or wrists (you can do push hands with one or both hands depending on your skill level) early on, and once contact has been established, it should never be broken, because this is how you read your opponent's intent.

While other styles of t'ai chi teach their students to yield and draw the opponent's force deep into their root, Hwa Yu students are taught that they can concentrate their chi into whichever part of their body is being attacked. This concentration of chi enables any part of the defender's body to be turned into a fist, which then enables the defender to simply roll the attack off and away from his or her body. Subsequently, the defender can then return the attackers advancing force right back into him or her by simply circling the energy and shifting that concentration of chi back from another angle. This technique is done by first bringing your internal energy into the part of your body that is being attacked, which will make that particular body part very hard, and then turning that body part in order to roll off the attack. In some cases, the circle can be continued so that the force goes right back into the attacker.

Another Push Hands method that is unique to Hwa Yu requires the practitioner to yield with any part of the body by making it soft and then rounding it so that the on coming attack will roll right off of it and be instantly neutralized.

Whenever we practice Push Hands within the Hwa Yu system we start out slowly and always keep safety in mind. It is not recommended to speed up until a student has the necessary safety precautions well mastered, because practicing at full speed with the Hwa Yu movements will certainly result in serious injury for one or both players if these precautions are not followed. While many t'ai chi schools hold Push Hands tournaments, this practice is not recommended for Hwa Yu students, because the quick hip sits and springlike motions could easily jar an opponent enough to cause severe injury.

# Recommended Reading

Dillon, Paul, "Basics of 6 Combinations 8 Methods Boxing." *Tai Chi Magazine,* Wayfarer Publications, 20:4 (1996): pp. 24–28.

Foxx, Khan. "Teachers and their Styles." Water Spirit 6x8. http://waterspirit6x8tripod// spirit/id18.html. 12/18/03.

Huang, Wen-Shan. *Fundamentals of Tai Chi Ch'uan.* Hong Kong: South Sky Book Company, 1974.

Li, John Chung and Li Tung Fung. *The Chinese Five Word Song.* Blountsville, Alabama: Fifth Estate, Inc., 2004.

Smallheiser, M., from an interview with Liu Jun. "Key Skills of Yang and Sun Styles." *Tai Chi Magazine,* Wayfarer Publications, 21:2 (April, 1997): pp. 6–10.

Wildman, Eugene, "Chen Po/Chen Hsi-I." Chinese Internal Martial Arts, Wai Lun Choi, http://www.liuhopaafa.com/chenpo.htm. 12/18/03

———. "Liu Ho Ba Fa." Chinese Internal Martial Arts, Wai Lun Choi, http://www.liuhopafa.com/art5.htm. 10/26/03.

Wolf, S. L., Barnhart, H. X., Kutner, N. G., McNeely, E., Coogler, C., Xu, T. Sponsored by Emery University School of Medicine. "Reducing Frailty and Falls in Older Persons." *The Journal of the American Geriatric Society,* 2:5 (May, 1996): pp. 599–600.

Xavier, Robert F. "Hwa Yu Tai-Chi Health and Wellbeing." Grace Martial Arts Fellowship, http://www.gmaf.org.

———. "A Lineage of Hwa Yu T'ai Chi." Grace Martial Arts Fellowship, http://www.gmaf.org.

———. "The History of Hwa Yu T'ai Chi." Grace Martial Arts Fellowship, http://www.gmaf.org.

———. "The Principles of Hwa Yu T'ai Chi." Grace Martial Arts Fellowship, http://www.gmaf.org.

Xu, H., Lawson, D., and Kras, A. "A Study on Tai Chi Exercises and Traditional Medical Maladies in the Relation to Bone Structure, Bone Function, and Menopausal Symptoms." *The Journal of Chinese Medicine* 74 (February, 2004): pp. 3–7.

# About the Author

Glenn Newth began his martial arts training in 1971 and has spent thirty-five years perfecting his art. He is a life-long martial arts professional and currently holds the rank of 8th degree black belt in Yon Ch'uan martial arts. In 1978 the noted Hwa Yu T'ai Chi Grand Master John Chung Li awarded him an instructor's certification in Hwa Yu T'ai Chi. In 2002, the current U.S. lineage holder, Master Robert Xavier, awarded Mr. Newth the title of Master in the art of Hwa Yu T'ai Chi, and named him successor to the lineage handed down from Master John Li. Mr. Newth has had extensive training in Aikido, Judo, Karate, and many of the weapons that are taught within those systems. He has also had training in Ninjitsu and Jujitsu. He has compiled an impressive record as a serious kata (forms) competitor, and is proficient in several weapons arts.

Mr. Newth has taught in many schools, both public and private, throughout New England and in various martial arts clubs in Connecticut. He was an instructor and board member for the Otis Ridge Camp for Martial Arts in Otis, Massachusetts, a summer children's camp specializing in martial arts.

He currently serves on the board of directors for the Yon Ch'uan Martial Arts Federation and resides in Connecticut with his son Cory.

# More Information

Master Xavier's Grace Martial Arts Fellowship (GMAF) has produced a series of videos and DVDs to help the Hwa Yu student better understand the exercises described in this book. For more information, please visit www.videotaichi.com.